THE
COCKTAIL
HANDBOOK

THE COCKTAIL HANDBOOK

DAVID BIGGS

PHOTOGRAPHY BY RYNO

NEW HOLLAND

First published in 1999 by New Holland Publishers Ltd
London ● Cape Town ● Sydney ● Auckland

24 Nutford Place
London W1H 6DQ
United Kingdom

14 Aquatic Drive
Frenchs Forest, NSW 2086
Australia

80 McKenzie Street
Cape Town 8001
South Africa

218 Lake Road
Northcote, Auckland
New Zealand

ISBN 1 85974 098 7 (h/b)

PROJECT MANAGER: Linda de Villiers
DESIGNER: Petal Palmer
DESIGN ASSISTANT: Lellyn Creamer
EDITOR: Annelene van der Merwe
PHOTOGRAPHER: Ryno
STYLIST: Sylvie Hurford
PROOFREADER AND INDEXER: Gail Jennings

Reproduction by Hirt & Carter Cape (Pty) Ltd
Printed and bound by Tien Wah Press (Pte) Ltd, Singapore

10 9 8 7 6 5 4 3 2 1

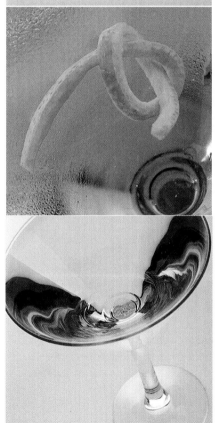

Photographic credits
ABPL: pp. 8, 9, 10 and 11; Four Roses Distillery: p.18;
Jack Daniel Distillery: p.110 top; Imperial Hotel, Tokyo p.14 and15;
Lanesborough Hotel, London: p.16 bottom left;
Magazine Features (Pty) Ltd: pp. 35 bottom right and 51;
Photofest: pp. 6, 27, 28, 33 bottom, 59, 67, 73, 76, 87, 109,
120, 132, 142 bottom, and 153; Raffles Hotel, Singapore: p.17;
The Robert Opie Collection pp. 57 and 77;
The Savoy Hotel, London: p.16 top; Unknown p.41

Photographer's and Publisher's acknowledgements
The photographer and the publishers wish to thank Banks Hiring Supply SA,
Buying Service SA (Pty) Ltd, Spilhaus WM Silverware (Pty) Ltd and The Yellow
Door for their generosity in supplying the glassware for the photography.

CONTENTS

INTRODUCTION

No-one knows for certain where the word "cocktail" originated, although many people have their favourite theories.

One theory is that the name was derived from a mixed drink called a "Coquetel", served to French officers in the southern States of America during the American War of Independence 1775 –1783.

Another theory is that the cocktail was the product of the American Prohibition era, but this is not so as cocktails were mentioned in a magazine article as far back as 1806, long before Prohibition was introduced.

The British claim the word comes from the dregs drawn from the very bottom of barrels of spirits and known as "cock-tailings".

My own favourite version is that they were the invention of an enterprising Irish-American innkeeper, Betsy Flanagan, who decorated her creations with gaily coloured feathers from fighting cocks. Apparently a very appreciative French customer found himself so delighted by his unusual drink that he raised his glass and toasted: "Vive le cocktail".

Whatever your own favourite tale, there is little doubt that the cocktail reached its peak of fame during the 1920s, when Prohibition was in full swing in America. (The one factor which did more to promote the popularity of the cocktail than any other was the enactment of the 18th Amendment to the American Constitution in 1919. It ushered in 13 years of total prohibition on the sale of alcoholic drinks in the United States of America.)

In order to stay one jump ahead of the beady-eyed police, the owners of "speakeasies" disguised the appearance of alcoholic drinks (and the rather rough taste of bad moonshine liquor), and the cocktail soared in popularity. And, of course, the fact that alcohol was illegal added to the glamour of the cocktail bar.

PROHIBITION

Prohibition was not an entirely new concept in the US. The State of Kansas had prohibited the sale of liquor back in the 1880s, becoming America's first "dry" state, and many other rural areas had vociferous groups that condemned the "demon alcohol" and demanded its total prohibition.

Moonshine was the name given to whisky distilled illicitly. In this photograph, barrels of the illegal alcohol have been confiscated to be destroyed.

"PROHIBITION makes
you want to cry into your
BEER, and then denies
you the beer to cry into."

Don Marquis

The ankle-flask became a fashion accessory in 1922. Here the little silver trinket is securely tucked away in these Russian boots.

Once the idea had been spread that the consumption of alcohol was a wicked and sinful thing, it was very difficult for any public figure to state openly that they approved of booze. It was tantamount to admitting that they condoned sinning.

So the Prohibitionists swept the board and the new law came into force in 1920, creating one of the most extraordinary periods of human history and – paradoxically – the birth of the "Cocktail Age". Give any commodity a rarity value and its price will rise. The more difficult it is to obtain, the more people will pay for it.

"Bootlegging" – the illegal sale of alcohol – became a lucrative business. The term "bootlegging" originated back in the old frontier days when it was illegal to sell alcohol to the native American Indians. Liquor smugglers used to slip bottles into the tops of their boots to carry them to their Indian customers.

The Prohibitionists underestimated the guile and greed of the people. Soon shiploads of illicit booze from Europe and South America were being landed on the coast and smuggled to hideaways throughout the United States. Profits were enormous.

The long coastline made it impossible to patrol the entire shore effectively, and the smugglers developed ingenious techniques to bring their wares ashore.

Liquor came ashore in garbage barges, fishing boats, sponge-diving vessels and anything else that floated and was unlikely to attract the attention of the US Coast Guard.

Incidentally, an interesting spin-off to the illicit liquor industry was the development of the American passion for "customizing" automobiles. Specialists were in great demand if they could make a car go faster than the vehicles used by the excisemen.

It was legal, in certain cases, to obtain a doctor's prescription for "medicinal" whisky and many doctors grew very rich writing out prescriptions for their ailing patients.

During Prohibition, alcohol was sold illegally in establishments known in the United States as "speakeasies", probably so named because the regulars would knock softly on the door and wait until the little slot was opened before speaking the password softly and being admitted. They "spoke easy" in order to get inside.

It was also possible to obtain permits to import denatured alcohol for industrial use, and it is estimated that some 57 million litres of this alcohol was diverted into the illegal drink industry during the years of Prohibition. It would first be cooked in an effort to drive off any poisonous chemicals, and then the bootlegger added his own recipe of flavouring and colouring agents to produce what was sold as "whiskey" or "gin" or "rum". Often it was extremely dangerous, resulting in illness, paralysis, blindness and even death.

But by the late 1920s the industry had become quite organised, and well-concealed, illegal stills had been established in many mountain and forest areas. Here, liquor was distilled from corn syrup, malt and yeast in a rather crude way, and the resulting booze was known to be dangerous. It was given names like "coffin varnish", "squirrel juice", "rotgut" and "strike-me-dead".

Sometimes it did.

This dreadful liquor was sold in speakeasies, and the most popular establishments were those that found ways of making it palatable. They mixed it with fruit juices, added syrups and decorated it with slices of fruit.

The cocktail was the only acceptable way to enjoy a drink. Bartenders became legends on the reputation of their cocktail recipes.

Of course, no lucrative industry like this remains untouched by crime for long, and soon organized gangs took over the distribution of illegal drink from the private entrepreneurs.

It was big money; it was a dangerous game. Gangsters fought and died protecting the right to

One of the most imaginative smuggling systems was used on the notorious schooner Rosie. *Filled with Scotch Malt, the torpedoes were sixteen feet long and two feet in diameter. At the top was an air chamber which allowed the torpedoes to float, and in this manner they could be towed in the water unseen.*

sell booze in their hard-won territories. Where competition raised its head, it was eliminated ruthlessly by gang bosses like the notorious Al Capone. It was only when Prohibition was repealed in 1933 that the liquor industry settled down to legal respectability and the gangs lost their reason to exist.

Whether they admit it or not, many of America's most wealthy and respectable families today owe their fortunes to the illegal trade in liquor. They have become respectable now, just as the cocktail has done.

Prohibition had played a valuable role in achieving exactly the opposite of what its protagonists had wanted. At the end of the Prohibition era, Americans were once again able to buy "normal" drinks that didn't require additives to mask the flavour, and cocktails declined in popularity. Who needs something that's freely available?

In recent years, however, the popularity of cocktails has grown once more and bartenders throughout the world are inventing new and tempting drinks to delight the palate and the eye. You may not find the word in your dictionary, but Americans now call an expert cocktail creator a "mixologist". Let's raise our glasses and drink a toast to the mixologists of the world.

The recipes in this book are for your guidance only. Experiment with proportions: a little more here and a little less there, depending on personal taste.

Don't be afraid to add a touch of sweetness, using grenadine or sugar syrup, or a hint of bitterness, using Angostura bitters, or a touch of sourness with lemon or lime juice. Anybody can read the standard recipe for a dry martini, but it takes an inspired bartender to create a truly memorable one.

We hope these pages will provide plenty of inspiration. Remember, though, that a great cocktail is not merely a way of getting as much alcohol as possible into your guest. It should be a treat for all the senses. A good cocktail looks good, smells good and tastes wonderful. A good cocktail balances the sweet with the sour, the sticky with the astringent. And, above all, it should stimulate good conversation and cement lasting friendships.

Cocktail recipes vary from bar to bar and this is as it should be. Every good bartender has his or her own recipes for classic cocktails. There are no "right" or "wrong" ways of making a drink, as long as it's the one you enjoy.

Some bartenders have the knack of finding exactly the right proportions to suit their particular customers. This is what makes them great.

In these chapters, you will find recipes for cocktails containing brandy, whisky, vodka, gin, rum and wine, as well as some of the new and exciting drinks available.

THE MEASURES

In this book we have tried to avoid using actual quantities when recording cocktail recipes. The reason for this is that almost every country has its own set of measurements. Some bartenders use gills, others use fluid ounces and still others measure their drinks in centilitres. If we had used conversions (take 2 oz/6 cl) the book would have become rather clumsy and confusing to the reader. It's far easier to work in proportion, we believe. "One part" of vodka to "two parts of orange juice" will taste just the same whether the parts are teaspoons, tot measures or buckets. By using proportions rather than quantities you can decide on the size of your drinks and also make up more than one at a time by substituting a coffee mug (or a bucket!) for your usual bar measuring jigger.

The cocktail is a uniquely American invention, so it's not surprising that good cocktail bars will usually be found where Americans gather to drink, whether it be at home or abroad.

During the American Prohibition era many sophisticated Americans enjoyed the freedom of travelling in Europe, where they could relax and imbibe alcoholic drinks without having to glance over their shoulders to see whether a stern police officer was taking down their names. Paris, Rome, Venice and other European capitals became the gathering places of the American intellectual crowd abroad, and where they went, cocktails followed.

It's an odd coincidence that two of the world's most famous cocktail bars are called "Harry's", but there's no direct connection between Harry's New York Bar in Paris and Harry's Bar in Venice. Their stories are fascinating.

Harry's New York Bar in Paris was founded by Harry MacElhone and became the meeting place of Americans living in Paris in the 1920s. Not only could they enjoy the imaginative cocktails from Harry's shaker, but it was one of the few places in France that served a good old American-style hot dog. Many cocktail classics, such as the Sidecar, have been attributed to Harry's inventive genius.

George Gershwin is alleged to have picked out the tune of "An American in Paris" while sitting at the downstairs piano of Harry's New York Bar. Gertrude Stein jotted down her poetry on Harry's tablecloths. Ernest Hemingway and F. Scott Fitzgerald were regulars at Harry's.

It was in this famous bar that Fernand Petiot, one of the bartenders, invented the Bloody Mary, starting a whole new family of spicy cocktails. Today the Bloody Mary is said to be the most popular vodka-based drink in America.

The other Harry's Bar was founded in kindness. A young American playboy, Harry Pickering, was living in Venice with his delightful maiden aunt and her gigolo. The three were regular customers at the bar of the Hotel Europa, where Guiseppe Cipriani wielded the magic cocktail shaker. After several months of happy and regular drinking, Harry suddenly stopped coming in for drinks.

One day Guiseppe met him and asked what was the matter. Was he ill? Did he no longer like the drinks at the Europa?

It turned out that Harry's parents had discovered he was living the high life of a playboy and had cut off his allowance. Suddenly he was broke.

Guiseppe advanced him $5000, a vast sum in those days, and Harry returned to America.

Two years later he returned to the Europa a wealthy man and repaid Guiseppe with liberal interest and a substantial cash gift in gratitude for his loan. With the money, Guiseppe was able to leave the Europa and start his own bar in what had been a rope warehouse. He named it

The Old Imperial Bar (above) at the Imperial Hotel in Tokyo, Japan, opened to the public in 1970. One of Frank Lloyd Wright's original architectural drawings (opposite) of the Imperial Hotel, which opened on the same day a devastating earthquake struck Tokyo and Yokohama on September 1st, 1923.

The American Bar (above) at The Savoy in London was opened by a bartender fleeing Prohibition in the 1930s. The Library Bar (left) in London's Lanesborough Hotel is presided over by Salvatore Calabrese, once chairman of the UK Bartender's Guild and Bartender of the Year in 1993.

"Harry's Bar" in honour of the young American who had made it possible. Today, the bar is run by Guiseppe's son, named Arrigo by parents who knew he would one day be in charge of Harry's. It must be the only instance in the world of a child being named after the bar he would one day own.

In 1934, after Prohibition had ended in America, the famous Petiot of Harry's New York Bar in Paris accepted an invitation to become the head barman at the Regis Hotel in New York. In due course the Regis Bar became almost as famous as Harry's had been.

Other bars to enjoy their moments of cocktail glory with the world's rich and famous include the Ritz in Paris, the American bar at the Savoy in London and the Long Bar at Raffles Hotel in Singapore.

And while the glitterati were enjoying the cocktail lifestyle in Europe, things were by no means dull in America. When Prohibition ended in 1933, the social action shifted from shady speakeasies to more glamorous nightclubs like the Stork Club, the El Morocco, Park Avenue Club and Morgan's.

Of course, cocktail bars are only as renowned as their bartenders, and the cocktail crowd tended to drift to where the best cocktails were reputed to be served. This is still the case today.

The earthy decor of the two-storey Long Bar – home of the Singapore Sling (page 57) – at Raffles Hotel in Singapore was inspired by Malayan plantations in the 1920s.

There are literally thousands of alcoholic drinks available to the enthusiastic bartender and nobody can be expected to stock every one of them, but as you increase your repertoire of cocktails, you'll wish to add new and different drinks to your stock.

Every bar should have a basic range of spirits, mixers and garnishes, which can be adapted to suit your own needs.

I have not listed wines in any detail here, because wines are a vast subject in themselves and can – and do – fill many books on their own. For the basic cocktail bar you should have a dry white wine and a serviceable red blend.

Here's a list of basics to act as a guide for the beginner bartender.

THE SPIRITS
Brandy or cognac
Gin
Vodka
Rum (dark and light)
Scotch whisky
Bourbon
Tequila
Vermouth, dry and sweet
Sparkling wine (dry)
Dry white wine (Sauvignon Blanc is a safe bet)

Dry red wine (an inexpensive blended red wine will do)
Triple Sec
Your own choice of liqueurs

THE MIXERS
Club soda
Colas
Ginger ale
Indian tonic water
Tomato juice
Fruit juices
Mineral water
Grenadine
Angostura bitters

SAUCES, SPICES AND GARNISHES
Maraschino cherries
Olives (green and black)
Cocktail onions
Lemons
Limes
Oranges
Nutmeg
Caster sugar
Tabasco sauce
Worcestershire sauce
Sugar syrup (gomme)
Sour syrup (a mixture of lemon
   and lime juice)

AND FINALLY
Ice, ice and more ice, cubes, crushed and cracked. You can never have too much ice in a good cocktail bar.

EQUIPMENT

For many readers, cocktails will be a passing fancy – a one-party stand – and there's nothing wrong with that. If this is what you are doing you'll probably find all the equipment you need already in your home. You can use ordinary kitchen tools and utensils to create almost any cocktail.

But for those who wish to take their cocktail making a little more seriously, it's worth getting a few accessories that will make your task much more enjoyable and certainly enhance your reputation as a host.

When selecting equipment, always try to buy good-quality items. They should look good, feel good and do the job for which they are designed. Here's a short list of items the budding home bartender would need.

A SHARP KNIFE

AN ICE BUCKET
The traditional ice bucket is made of metal, but in hot climates it might be better to have one with an insulated lining.

ICE TONGS

A MEASURE
It doesn't really matter what size measure you use, as long as you use the same one for all the ingredients of your drink; they are also known as "jiggers" or "tot measures". It may be a good idea to have two measures, one being twice the capacity of the other.

CORKSCREWS
There are many different kinds available. There is the "screwpull" range, which has the spirals with a non-stick coating; the "waiter's friend", which has an arm that rests on the rim of the bottle to provide leverage; the "wing" corkscrew, which has two arms that are depressed to lift the cork from the bottle neck; the "Ah So", which is a cork lifter rather than a corkscrew, with two slender prongs of spring steel that are slid down the sides of the cork and then carefully twisted out (it is designed to handle corks that have become crumbly with age); and the "cork pump", a hand-operated pump attached to a hollow needle which is pushed down through the cork.

A BOTTLE OPENER

A COCKTAIL SHAKER

A BAR GLASS WITH STRAINER

A WATER PITCHER

The following are useful if mixing drinks in substantial quantities.

A BAR SPOON

CLOTHS

BAR TOWELS

DAMP WIPING CLOTH

GLASSES

Cocktail purists will throw up their hands in horror if they see a drink being served in the "wrong" kind of glass. Martinis, they will tell you, should be served only in martini glasses, and a Harvey Wallbanger in anything but a highball glass would be a mortal sin. In today's more relaxed age, however, we tend to be less rigid about our choice of glasses.

There's a wide range of glasses available for cocktails and it probably isn't necessary to have sets of all of them in your cocktail bar. For all practical purposes you should get by with just four designs – the highball, the lowball, the champagne flute and the cocktail glass. One of the basic guidelines should be the stronger the drink, the smaller the glass.

THE SHOT GLASS (1)
This small glass is used to serve a drink with a very high alcohol content, and for those colourful little "shooters" that are meant to be downed in a single, throat-searing gulp.

THE COCKTAIL GLASS (2)
This is an elegant little glass with a shallow, flared bowl, and a stem to prevent your hand warming the chilled drink too much

THE MARTINI GLASS (3)
Probably the best known and most often photographed of all cocktail glasses, it is used for martinis and margaritas.

THE BRANDY BALLOON (4)
Designed to provide the brandy in it with a very large surface area to allow the aroma to rise, it has a rather narrow mouth to gather the aroma and concentrate it for maximum impact.

PORT AND SHERRY GLASSES (5)
These miniature wineglasses are designed to take a small amount of fortified wine.

THE CHAMPAGNE SAUCER (6)
Totally impractical for champagne, as it allows the bubbles to dissipate too quickly, it is suitable for certain cocktails such as Russian Coffee (page 84).

THE CHAMPAGNE FLUTE (7)
This elegantly slim glass is perfect for any champagne-based drink, or, in fact, anything with bubbles in it. The tall, clear glass shows off the bubbles to best effect as they rise slowly up the column, and the small surface area ensures that the bubbles do not disappear too fast.

THE LOWBALL GLASS (8)
This is often used for Bloody Marys and other drinks that have a large proportion of mixer to alcohol.

THE HIGHBALL GLASS (9)
This taller version of the lowball glass is intended for long drinks like fruit punches and Harvey Wallbangers.

THE PARIS GOBLET (10)
This is the standard wineglass. It is also sometimes used for drinks like pink gin.

DECORATING YOUR DRINKS

One of the charming things about cocktails is that they are designed to please all the senses. They should not only taste good but smell good and look good as well. And the tinkle of ice in the glass certainly sounds good.

The conscientious bartender will take care to ensure that his or her creations are a feast for the eye as well as the palate, but the garnish should never dominate the cocktail. A concoction bristling with fruit, paper umbrellas, plastic swizzle sticks and bright-blue plastic ice cubes simply looks a mess.

By adding just the right touch of garnish, however, a clever bartender can give an indication of the flavour to be expected. A twist of lemon or lime, for example, tells the drinker to be prepared for a crisp, slightly tangy drink. A maraschino cherry on a cocktail stick or a ball of pink watermelon would indicate something sweet and syrupy.

Some garnishes, like a sprig of mint, actually add to the flavour or aroma of the drink, while there are certain cocktails that traditionally include a specific garnish, like the olive in a dry martini.

A pretty touch can be added by serving the cocktail in a glass with a frosted rim. This is usually done by wetting the rim of the glass, either with water or egg white, and then dipping it carefully into a saucer of fine sugar; the sugar sticks to the moistened edge.

In the case of a margarita, the rim of the glass is traditionally frosted with salt.

Some drinks are best sipped through a straw, and unless the glass is a tall one, a short straw is best. Trim off as much of a full-length straw as you require.

THE ROLE OF FRUIT

Many cocktail recipes call for fruit, and even some of those that don't can be enhanced by the addition of a slice of fresh fruit dropped into the glass, or a chunk of fruit threaded onto a cocktail stick, if the mood is right.

Fruit can play a number of roles in the creation of the perfect cocktail for the occasion. Remember that a good cocktail should not only taste good but look good too. And fruit is ideal for adding eye appeal.

Appropriate fruits, when in season, can provide an exciting base for a cocktail. Bananas, melons, peaches, apricots and all sorts of soft fruit can be liquidized in a blender to create a delicious fruit purée. Vodka, rum or brandy added to it gives you a superb drink.

The photograph opposite will provide inspiration when you're creating a new drink.

"O God, that **men** should

put an enemy in their mouths

to steal away their BRAINS!"

William Shakespeare, *Othello*

Sooner or later the enthusiastic drinker will encounter this demon: the hangover. Chances are you'll blame it on the soda water, the peanuts or the suspect quality of the cheese straws – but seldom, if ever, on the alcohol you consumed the night before.

It's interesting to see how many drinkers claim they cannot handle champagne because it "gives them such a hangover". But just think of the occasions when we drink champagne. These are usually celebrations – weddings, birthdays, engagements and so on. And the evening often begins with a beer or two, continues with a few cocktails and a glass or two of wine with the meal, and then, when it comes to speech time, we break out the champagne to drink the toasts. And we always blame the champers, not the beers or the cocktails or wine, for the hangover we inevitably suffer the following morning.

The hangover is a malady as old as alcohol itself and many cures have been prescribed. Few of them actually work, but when you're feeling as dreadful as that, you'll try anything. Even death seems a happy alternative to the pounding, sick head and stomach of a hangover.

One of the worst aspects of a hangover is that it seldom evokes much sympathy from anybody else. There's a general attitude of "well, you have only yourself to blame".

This may be perfectly true, but it's not the sort of statement that makes the sufferer feel any better. In the throes of a hangover we need sympathy and understanding and – above all – total silence.

The ancient Egyptians believed boiled cabbage would do the trick. The Assyrians recommended ground-up swallows' beaks blended with myrrh. Where one was supposed to find a swallow's beak the morning after a rough party history does not relate.

In South America some ancient Indian tribes believed the best remedy was to tie the sufferer tightly in his hammock like a mummy and leave him alone until he was ready to face the world.

I believe the old Scots thought the best way was to wrap the patient tightly in an oxhide and stow him out of sight behind a waterfall.

Many famous authors' have described their own hangover remedies.

Thackeray wrote: "To this truth I can vouch as a man; there is no headache in the world like that caused by Vauxhall Punch." He does not describe the punch in detail, but later writes: "Small beer was the only drink with which unhappy gentlemen soothed the fever of their previous night's potation."

Small beer was beer made by adding water to the mash left after the real beer had been brewed, and fermenting it a second time. It was a thin and cheap drink, and rather watery.

Norma Shearer (above) *in The Divorcee.*
Marlene Dietrich (previous page) *looking the worse for wear in Blonde Venus.*

Lord Byron, in his epic satire *Don Juan*, says:

"Get very drunk; and when
You wake with a headache, you shall see what then.
Ring for your valet – bid him quickly bring
Some hock and soda water, then you'll know
A pleasure worth Xerxes, the greatest king;
For not the blest sherbert, sublimed with snow,
Nor the first sparkle of the desert spring,
Nor Burgundy in all its sunset glow
After long travel, ennui, love or slaughter,
Vie with that draught of hock and soda water."

In fact, Byron's writing about the drink we call a "spritzer" today. Not a bad idea.

Some people believe there's merit in the old "hair of the dog that bit you" story. In other words, cure the malady with a quick shot of whatever caused it. This, of course, raises serious problems if you were bitten by a whole pack of dogs of different breeds.

Some hangover sufferers recommend such odd mixtures as raw egg liberally laced with Worcestershire sauce.

Actress Tallulah Bankhead recommended Black Velvet, a mixture of champagne and stout, as a hangover cure, but adds, rather honestly: "Don't be swindled into believing there's any cure for a hangover. I've tried them all. Time alone can stay it."

In his book *Clement Freud's Book of Hangovers*, British ex-politician, chef and *bon viveur* Clement Freud makes the following suggestion: "Drink plenty of water, milk or fruit juice before, during and after drinking alcohol."

Plenty of water certainly helps relieve the suffering, and a couple of paracetamol tablets swallowed immediately before going to bed – if you can remember, at that fuzzy stage of the evening, to take them – definitely reduces the pain the following morning.

In America the Prairie Oyster (see recipe opposite) is recommended.

Frankly, if you can look a Prairie Oyster in the eye when you have a hangover, you're a better man than I am.

Here are a few recipes. Read them while you're sober.

PICK-ME-UP GENTLY

This very gentle drink for the morning after is unlikely to cause any further damage. It is non-alcoholic and many users swear that it settles the stomach as fast as anything else they've tried (which may be damning with faint praise, but it's worth a try).

Ice cubes
The juice of half a lemon
Two teaspoons of Worcestershire sauce
Soda water

- Place two ice cubes in a highball glass (oh, any glass will do as long as it's handy without any fuss) and add the lemon juice and Worcestershire sauce.
- Top up with soda water and sip very quietly.
- Avoid human contact.

POLYNESIAN PICK-ME-UP

Here again, we rely on savoury flavours combined with tart, acid fruit juices to affect a cure. Look, nobody is saying these are pleasant drinks. They are, essentially, medicine.

Crushed ice
One part vodka
Four parts fresh pineapple juice
Half a teaspoon of curry powder
A teaspoon of lemon juice
Two dashes of Tabasco sauce
Cayenne pepper

- Place half a cup of crushed ice and all the ingredients except the cayenne pepper in a blender.
- Blend for about 10 seconds and pour it into a lowball glass.
- Dust the surface lightly with cayenne pepper and drink it in a single, shuddering gulp.

PRAIRIE OYSTER

The Prairie Oyster, sometimes called the Mountain Oyster, is one of the oldest hangover remedy cocktails around, although the strong flavours are daunting to some.

Ice cubes
One generous measure of brandy
Two teaspoons of cider vinegar
A dessertspoon of Worcestershire sauce
A teaspoon of tomato sauce (catsup)
Half a teaspoon of Angostura bitters
The yolk of a fresh egg
Cayenne pepper

- Place five ice cubes in a cocktail shaker and add the brandy, vinegar, Worcestershire sauce, tomato sauce and bitters.
- Strain it into a lowball glass and add ice cubes to bring it to the top of the glass.
- Carefully float the unbroken yolk of the egg on top of the drink and sprinkle it lightly with cayenne pepper.
- Traditionally this concoction should be downed in a single, brave gulp. You're welcome to try it.

BRANDY

Brandy, that warming spirit distilled from wine, is produced in many

forms around the world. Best known are the heady cognacs and armagnacs of France (probably

considered by purists to be too noble to be used in anything as frivolous as a cocktail), but fine brandy

is also distilled in many other countries, including Germany, Greece, America and South Africa.

Top-quality brandies are produced in copper pot stills, while the more commercial brands are made

in continuous patent stills. Several countries have regulations stating what proportion of a brandy may

be produced in a continuous still and how long the distilled product must be matured in oak vats before

being released for sale.

The tradition of maturing brandy in oak goes back to the 15th century, when an alchemist allegedly

took his precious barrel of aqua vitae and buried it in his yard to keep it out of the hands of soldiers

about to attack his village. The poor man died in the attack and it was only years later that the barrel was discovered. Half the liquor had evaporated by then, but the remaining nectar was found to be incredibly rich and smooth.

Brandy has long been considered a man's drink. Samuel Johnson's 18th-century philosophy was: "Claret is the liquor for boys, port for men: but he who aspires to be a hero must drink brandy." Times have certainly changed, and today brandy is a spirit enjoyed as much by woman as by men.

Brandy is a surprisingly versatile drink that mixes well with a very wide range of other flavours, as these recipes will demonstrate.

"ALCOHOL removes warts.

Not from me –

from whomever I'm with."

Jackie Gleason

B & B is a natural blend of brandy and Benedictine, a herb-flavoured brandy liqueur made in Normandy, France.

B & B

This is a natural combination, as Benedictine is a herb-flavoured liqueur based on brandy and originally made by Benedictine monks who claimed it had fine medicinal qualities, which it probably does.

Ice cubes
One part brandy
One part Benedictine
A twist of lime

- Place two or three ice cubes in a bar glass and add the brandy and Benedictine.
- Stir well and strain into a small cocktail glass.
- Garnish with the twist of lime.

B & B COLLINS

The B & B can be extended to make a
B & B Collins simply by adding soda, but that
would be very unadventurous. Rather, try this
little variation.

Two parts brandy
The juice of half a lemon
A teaspoon of sugar syrup
Crushed ice
Club soda water
One part Benedictine
A slice of lemon

◈ Mix the brandy, lemon juice and sugar syrup
   in a bar glass after adding three scoops of
   crushed ice.
◈ Strain it into a chilled lowball glass and top
   with soda water.
◈ Now carefully float the Benedictine on the
   surface and garnish with the slice of lemon.

*B & B Collins (above right), a longer, cooler
variation of the B & B, and Blacksmith
Cocktail (above left), a smooth blend of
Drambuie and crème de café.*

BLACKSMITH COCKTAIL

There's a rough Irish drink called a "Blacksmith"
which consists, predictably, of half a pint each of
Guinness stout and barley wine, probably best
drunk in the glow of the blacksmith's forge. Our
Blacksmith Cocktail, however, is better suited to
the cocktail bar.

Ice cubes
One part brandy
One part Drambuie
One part crème de café

◈ Place four or five ice cubes in a bar mixing
   glass, add all the ingredients and stir well.
◈ Serve on the rocks in a lowball glass
   or a whisky glass, ungarnished.

*Edward Everett Horton and Irene Hervey in a
happy scene from* His Night Out.

BRANDY COCKTAIL

There must be dozens of cocktails called, simply, "Brandy Cocktail". One bartender's reference book on my shelf contains no fewer than eight completely different brandy cocktails.

Here are two of my favourites for you to try:

VERSION 1

Ice cubes

One part brandy

One part dry vermouth

A dash of Angostura bitters

Lemon zest

A cocktail cherry

* Place five ice cubes in a bar mixing glass and add the brandy, vermouth and bitters.
* Stir gently and strain into a cocktail glass.
* Add the lemon zest.
* Garnish with a cocktail cherry on a stick.

VERSION 2

Ice cubes

Two parts brandy

One part vermouth

One part Grand Marnier

Angostura bitters

Orange peel

* Place four or five ice cubes in a bar mixing glass and pour the brandy, vermouth and Grand Marnier over them. Stir well.
* Add two dashes of bitters to an empty cocktail glass and swirl it round to coat the inside of the glass.

* Strain the mixture from the mixing glass into the cocktail glass.
* Squeeze the orange peel over the glass to add zest and aroma.
* Serve ungarnished.

THE SIDECAR

The 1920s, the golden age of the cocktail, was also the golden age of motoring. The novelty of the horseless carriage had not yet worn off and automobiles were different and dashing. And the most dashing of all the knights of the road were the gallant fellows who dared to ride motorcycles.

The Sidecar is said to be named after a rather eccentric military man who used to arrive at Harry's New York Bar in Paris in the sidecar of a chauffeur-driven motorcycle.

Ice cubes

One and a half parts brandy

One part Cointreau

One part fresh lemon juice (or more to taste)

◈ Place four ice cubes in a mixing glass, pour the ingredients over the ice and stir well.

◈ Strain into a cocktail glass and serve.

The brandy cocktail (above centre and right) comes in several versions. It's fun to find your own favourite. The Sidecar (above left) is one of many cocktail classics that had its origins in the legendary Harry's New York Bar in Paris (right).

BULL'S MILK

Milk is traditionally the drink for children, so it is unlikely that the rough, tough gangsters of the Prohibition era would have accepted it willingly. But Bull's Milk is another matter. The bull is the symbol of bravery and awesome power – and no macho male could quibble with a glass of that.

Ice cubes

One part brandy

One cup of milk

Sugar syrup to taste

Grated nutmeg

Ground cinnamon

◈ Place four or five ice cubes in a cocktail shaker and add the brandy, milk and sugar syrup to taste.

◈ Shake the mixture well and strain it into a highball glass.

◈ Sprinkle the nutmeg and cinnamon over it and serve immediately.

Brandy puts the fiery spirit into Bull's Milk (left), a drink fit for a matador.

STINGER

This very old cocktail recipe has its origins in the days of American Prohibition and has become a true classic. Originally it was served "straight up" but most people now prefer to sip it on the rocks. It's a good way to get a party rolling as fast as possible; one or two Stingers and your guests are almost guaranteed to be in a jolly mood.

Ice cubes

Two parts brandy

One part white crème de menthe

- Place six ice cubes in a cocktail shaker and add the brandy and crème de menthe.
- Shake well and strain into a chilled cocktail glass.
- Serve ungarnished or with a sprig of mint.

"Drink has caused many a lady **to be** loved that otherwise might have died single."

Finley Peter Dunne

The clean, minty flavour of the Stinger (right) makes it a superb drink to serve before or at the end of a good meal.

EGGNOG

Traditionally this was the drink served in English country homes on Christmas morning to keep out the chill. The eggnog probably derived its name from the term "noggin", which was a small glass of strong beer. Some folk enjoyed this with an egg beaten in to thicken it. Nowadays we prefer brandy and rum instead of beer. It's one of the few cocktails in this collection that does not involve ice.

One part brandy
One part dark rum
One fresh egg
A dash of sweet syrup
Five parts full-cream milk
Whole nutmeg

- Place the brandy, rum, egg and syrup in a shaker and shake vigorously to create a creamy consistency.
- Strain it into a highball glass, add the milk and stir it gently.
- Grate a sprinkling of nutmeg over it and serve at room temperature.

Eggnog (left) is a drink that will warm the chilliest of winter mornings – you may even use warm milk.

THE INTERNATIONAL

One of the reasons this cocktail got its name is that it combines the flavours typical of several national drinks.

Crushed ice
Two parts cognac
Half a part vodka
Half a part ouzo
Half a part Cointreau

* Place two scoops of crushed ice in a bar mixing glass and add the cognac, vodka, ouzo and Cointreau.
* Stir well and strain into a chilled cocktail glass.
* Serve ungarnished, or decorate with a tiny flag.

The International is a blend of traditional flavours: vodka from Russia, cognac and Cointreau from France and ouzo from Greece.

"And Noah he often said to his wife

when he sat down to DINE

'I don't care where the water goes

if it doesn't get into the WINE.' "

G. K. Chesterton

Rolls Royce (left front), a cocktail as elegant as the car after which it is named, and Steeplejack (left back), a long, cool drink with a distinct apple flavour.

France, better known for its legendary Cognac and Armagnac spirits, produces fine brandies in other regions, too (see poster opposite). Almost every wine producing area in the world has a brandy tradition as well.

STEEPLEJACK

Calvados is distilled apple cider and is a popular spirit in parts of France, such as Normandy, where apple cider is the drink of the area. In other parts of the world it is sold as apple brandy or applejack.

One part Calvados (oh, okay, applejack then)
One and a half parts chilled apple juice
One and a half parts soda water
One teaspoon of lime juice
Ice cubes
A slice of lemon

◆ Pour the Calvados, apple juice, soda water and lime juice into a bar glass and stir gently.
◆ Pour the mixture into a highball glass and add enough ice to fill it.
◆ Garnish with a slice of lemon.

THE ROLLS ROYCE

Perhaps this drink was designed to be served in the back of a Rolls as the chauffeur drives you silently through the British countryside.

Crushed ice
One part cognac
One part Cointreau
One part orange juice

◆ Place three scoops of crushed ice in a cocktail shaker and add the cognac, Cointreau and orange juice.
◆ Shake well, then strain the contents into a chilled cocktail glass.
◆ Serve ungarnished.

**"You say alcohol is slow poison?
So, who's in a hurry?"**

Robert Benchley

SAUVION'S

CHARLESTON

The Charleston was one of the most popular dances during the Prohibition era and typified the new, rather risqué age, when young ladies could show an ankle in public and dresses were figure-hugging and sheer rather than elaborate and all-concealing. This drink would have appealed to the liberated young women of the time. It appeals just as much today.

One part mandarin Napoleon liqueur

One part cherry brandy

Ice cubes

Lemonade to taste

◈ Place the mandarin Napoleon and cherry brandy in a bar glass and stir well.

◈ Fill a highball glass with ice cubes and pour the cocktail over them.

◈ Top up with lemonade and serve.

The Charleston was named after one of the most popular dances during the Prohibition era.

WIDOW'S KISS

The spirit distilled from apple cider in the New England area of America is known as applejack. It is more or less the same as Calvados from France and has a hefty alcohol content of about 45%.

Crushed ice
One part applejack
One part Benedictine
Half a part yellow chartreuse
A dash of Angostura bitters
A fresh strawberry

❖ Place a scoop of crushed ice in a cocktail shaker and add the applejack, Benedictine, chartreuse and bitters.
❖ Shake well, strain into a chilled cocktail glass and float the fresh strawberry on the top.

Widow's Kiss is a potent brew of applejack and Benedictine, which sets one wondering what happened to the widow's late husband.

"**Claret** is the liquor for boys, port for men; but he who aspires to be a hero must drink **brandy**."

Samuel Johnson

OLD OXFORD UNIVERSITY PUNCH

Most of the Oxford academic year is in winter when the air is chilly in the draughty old college buildings. No doubt many a long and otherwise boring tutorial has been made more bearable by a warming mug of punch.

One cup of brown sugar
Boiling water
Three cups of lemon juice
One bottle of cognac
One bottle of dark Demerara rum
Cinnamon sticks and whole cloves

- Dissolve the sugar in the boiling water in a saucepan on low heat on the stove. Keep it hot, but ensure it does not boil at any stage. Add the lemon juice and cognac when the sugar has dissolved.
- Pour in almost all the rum, leaving about half a cup in the bottle.
- Shortly before serving, place the remaining rum in a ladle and heat over a flame. Light the rum in the ladle, pour the flaming spirit onto the surface of the punch and serve. If the flames are still flickering, extinguish them with the lid of the saucepan.

Old Oxford University Punch was designed to keep out the chill.

APPLE GINGER PUNCH

Ginger has been used in many drinks to add a glowing touch of spicy warmth. Here we combine the flavours of ginger beer and ginger wine to make a most refreshing party drink.

A large block of ice
One bottle of Calvados
Half a cup of maraschino liqueur
Half a cup of Kirsch
A bottle of ginger wine
Three cups of pineapple or grapefruit juice
Four apples (red or green)
Three bottles of ginger beer

- Place the ice in a punch bowl and pour the Calvados, maraschino, Kirsch, ginger wine and fruit juice over it.
- Cut the apples into wedge-shaped slices and float them in the punch.
- Shortly before serving, add the ginger beer to the bowl.

"There are TWO reasons for drinking: one is when you are thirsty, to cure it, the other is when you are not thirsty, to prevent it."

Thomas Love Peacock

Apple Ginger Punch, a cheerful and refreshing party punch, is filled with apple flavour from several sources and ginger to give it an exciting little bite.

G I N

Gin is probably the most commonly used base for cocktails, including the

most famous cocktail of them all the martini. The original gin used in Prohibition cocktails was known as

bathtub gin, as it was often concocted illegally in the bathtub and bore little if any resemblance to the

elegantly fragrant gin we know today. It was probably the dreadful flavour of those crude gins that gave

cocktails their popularity. Nobody could possibly have endured it neat.

Official definitions of gin describe it as a "neutral, rectified spirit distilled from any grain, potato or

beet and flavoured with juniper". This would seem to give the distillers a fairly wide range of possibilities

and indeed, there are several styles of the white spirit, all falling under the general category of "gin".

Each producer has a closely guarded recipe for gin, with juniper berries as a base,

but sometimes also including a touch of coriander, angelica root and seed, dried orange and lemon

peel, cassia bark and orris powder.

Sloe gin is one of the better-known styles of gin and has been flavoured with sloe, which is the small, dark fruit of the blackthorn. The name lends itself to some interesting and sometimes risqué cocktails, like the 'Sloe, Comfortable Screw" which is, of course, made up of sloe gin, Southern Comfort and the basic screwdriver ingredients.

There are probably as many variations of the popular martini as there are bartenders. Each

The Martini

A *whole book* could be written about the martini, which seems to embody the very *spirit of cocktails* and the American way of life.

one seems to have his or her own recipe and most enthusiasts will declare their own the only one worth drinking. The question, too, is whether a martini should be shaken or stirred. Here are a few variations of that famous cocktail.

MEDIUM MARTINI

If you use the same measure, this one will end up rather more alcoholic than the other two. Traditionally this elegant cocktail is served without any garnish.

Ice cubes
One part gin
One part dry vermouth
One part sweet vermouth

- Place eight ice cubes in a cocktail mixing glass and pour the gin and both measures of vermouth over them.
- Stir well and strain into a martini glass.

DRY MARTINI

The dry martini is undoubtedly the most famous cocktail in the world and every bartender has a favourite way of making it. This is just one of many martini variations.

Ice cubes
One part gin
One part dry vermouth
A green olive

- Place four ice cubes in a bar glass and add the gin and dry vermouth.
- Stir, then strain into a martini glass.
- Garnish with the olive on a cocktail stick.

SWEET MARTINI

Although the Dry Martini is considered the most sophisticated, the Sweet Martini has a friendly charm of its own.

Ice cubes

One part gin

One part sweet vermouth

A cocktail cherry

◈ Place eight ice cubes in a cocktail mixing glass.

◈ Add the gin and sweet vermouth.

◈ Stir well and strain into a martini glass.

◈ Garnish with the cocktail cherry on a cocktail stick.

Above from left to right: Dry Martini, Medium Martini, Sweet Martini. Martinis come in many forms – the difference is usually in the sweetness of the vermouth and the right choice of garnish.

The Montgomery (above left and centre) was invented by Ernest Hemingway in honour of the famous British general of World War II. The Cardinale (above right) is another of Harry's famous, gin-based cocktails and could be called a martini with a difference.

MONTGOMERY

This is a variation of the martini, originally invented by Ernest Hemingway in Harry's Bar in Venice. It was during World War II and Hemingway claimed Field-Marshall Montgomery would fight the enemy only if he had 15 soldiers to every one of theirs. He decided this was a good proportion of gin to vermouth.

Today Harry's version is slightly modified and has become a speciality of the bar.

Ten parts gin

One part dry vermouth

- Mix the gin and vermouth in a bar glass and pour into as many martini glasses as you are preparing.
- Place them in a freezer and leave until frozen solid.
- Serve frozen, so they can be sipped very slowly as they thaw.

CARDINALE

This cocktail has become so popular that it is available in bottled form, ready-mixed, all over America and Europe.

Six parts gin
One part dry vermouth
Three parts Campari
Ice cubes

- In a bar glass, stir together the gin, vermouth and Campari with three ice cubes.
- Strain into a cocktail glass and serve ungarnished.

TOM COLLINS

Many people refer to this drink as a "John Collins" and this is understandable. The original Collins was indeed a John, the head waiter at Limmer's Hotel in London in the 18th century. He is reputed to have used the rather heavy and oily Dutch-style gin in his drink, which was not very popular in America. One barman decided to use a London brand of gin called Old Tom in the cocktail instead. The drink gained popularity instantly and became known as the Tom Collins.

One part dry gin
One or two dashes of sugar syrup
The juice of one lemon
Soda water
Ice cubes
A slice of lemon

- Pour the gin, sugar syrup and lemon juice into a highball glass and stir it with a swizzle stick.
- Top up the glass with chilled soda water, add an ice cube if required and garnish with a slice of lemon.

The famous Harry's Bar in Venice (left) *run by Arrigo Cipriani, was the birthplace of Ernest Hemingway's Montgomery cocktail* (page 50).

THE BLUE ARROW

In the normal course of events, we hardly ever eat or drink anything that is blue, so a glass of blue liquid immediately conjures up visions of something new and exciting.

Crushed ice

Two parts gin

One part Cointreau

One part lime juice cordial

One part blue Curaçao

◆ Place about two cups of crushed ice in a cocktail shaker.

◆ Pour in the gin, Cointreau, lime juice and blue Curaçao and shake vigorously for about five seconds.

◆ Strain into a chilled cocktail glass and serve ungarnished.

PINK GIN

While we are on the subject of pretty colours for drinks, let's take a look at that very English drink, Pink Gin. The famous round-the-world sailor Sir Francis Chichester claims that it was Pink Gins that kept him cheerful (dare we say in good spirits) during his epic voyage.

The British do it the simple way. They just shake a couple of dashes of Angostura bitters into a glass, swirl it about to coat the inside and then add a dollop of gin.

Americans tend to prefer a slightly more precise version.

Ice cubes

Two dashes of Angostura bitters

Two measures of dry gin

A twist of lemon peel (optional)

◆ Place four ice cubes in a bar glass and add the bitters.

◆ Pour in the gin and stir well. Strain into a chilled cocktail glass.

◆ Usually served ungarnished, but you could add a twist of lemon peel for decoration.

"Candy is dandy but liquor is QUICKER."

Ogden Nash

Blue drinks have an exciting aura. Try the Blue Arrow (above left) and capture some of the mystery. The Tom Collins (above right) was originally made with heavy Dutch gin. Today, the lighter style of London gin is preferred.

A sweeter version of this classic cocktail, Bronx, can be made by substituting some or all of the dry vermouth with sweet vermouth.

BRONX

In the wild and naughty days of Prohibition each area was controlled by a different gang boss and booze played an important role in the economy of the underworld. Different areas of New York became known for the special drinks they offered. This one was the speciality of the Bronx.

The secondary ingredients were probably a desperate attempt to disguise the taste of the home-made bathtub gin. Modern gin, however, turns it into an elegant treat.

Ice cubes

Three parts gin

One part fresh orange juice

One part dry vermouth

◈ Place four or five ice cubes in a cocktail shaker. Add the gin, orange juice and vermouth and shake well.

◈ Strain into a cocktail glass and serve ungarnished.

GIN FIZZ

This is a long, cooling drink made famous in magazine articles published as long ago as the 1870s.

Ice cubes

A large measure of gin

The juice of half a lemon

A dash of sweet gomme syrup

One egg

Soda water

A slice of lemon

◈ Place four ice cubes in a cocktail shaker and add the gin, lemon juice and gomme syrup.

◈ Crack the egg and add the yolk or white, depending on your choice of fizz, to the shaker.

◈ Shake vigorously for 30 seconds and strain it into a highball glass.

◈ Top it up with chilled soda water and garnish with a slice of lemon.

The Singapore Sling (above left) was first served in Raffles Hotel in Singapore in 1915. The addition of the white of an egg to a Gin Fizz (above right) gives it a silver fizz; the yolk would make it golden.

The Maiden's Prayer is reputed to mend broken hearts and is said to have been invented to soothe a young lady customer who was crying at the bar after her romance had been shattered.

SINGAPORE SLING

This cocktail became a firm favourite of writers such as Joseph Conrad and Somerset Maugham. It was an elaborate concoction designed to please female drinkers, but was soon modified and enjoyed by cocktail lovers of both sexes.

Here's a simplified and more practical version of the original, which contained no less than eight ingredients.

Ice cubes
Two parts dry gin
One part cherry brandy
One part fresh lemon juice
Soda water
A slice of lemon
A maraschino cherry

- Place four ice cubes in a cocktail shaker and add the gin, cherry brandy and lemon juice.
- Shake well and strain into a highball glass.
- Top up with soda water and garnish with the slice of lemon and the cherry on a cocktail stick.

"I NEVER DRINK anything stronger than GIN before breakfast."

W. C. Fields

This label was designed c.1870 and has a space in which the distributor's or distiller's name can be inserted.

MAIDEN'S PRAYER

Oranges and lemons are traditionally associated with purity and innocence, which is why orange blossoms are often used as wedding cake decoration. Maybe this is part of the reason for this drink's name.

Ice cubes
One part gin
One part Cointreau
Half a part orange juice
Half a part lemon juice

- Place three or four ice cubes in a cocktail shaker and add the gin, Cointreau, orange juice and lemon juice.
- Shake well and strain into a cocktail glass.

GIMLET

A gimlet is a small, sharp spike used for drilling holes, usually twisted into wood to make a pilot hole for a screw. When you think about it, gimlet is an appropriate name for a small, sharp drink with a twist to it.

Ice cubes

Two parts gin

One part lime juice cordial

A twist of lime rind

◆ Place two or three ice cubes in a cocktail mixing glass. Add the gin and lime juice cordial and stir well.

◆ Strain over ice cubes in a lowball glass and garnish with the twist of lime.

GIN AND TONIC

In the far-flung outposts of the British Empire malaria was a constant danger and quinine was often used as an antidote. It didn't take Her Majesty's servants long to discover that quinine tonic flavoured with a dash of gin made a dashed fine sundowner.

Ice cubes

A generous measure of dry gin

Tonic water

A slice of lemon

◆ Place three ice cubes in a tall glass. Splash in a liberal measure of gin and top up the glass with tonic.

◆ Drop in a slice of lemon, twisted to release some of the zest.

◆ Stir gently before serving.

Gin and Tonic (far left) has been a favourite drink wherever the British forces have raised the imperial flag. The Gimlet (left) is one of the true classics of the cocktail world and there are about as many individual versions as there are of the equally famous martini. Joan Crawford (opposite) accepts a drink from Nils Asther in Letty Lynton.

Named after the famous French field gun, the French 75 is another classic cocktail from Harry's New York Bar in Paris.

FRENCH 75

Cocktails have been made to celebrate all kinds of events and commemmorate all sorts of things. In World War 1 the French light field gun, known as the '75', was regarded as one of the world's most formidable weapons. After the War, when veterans gathered in Harry's New York Bar in Paris, a special cocktail was devised to remember the fierce field gun.

One part chilled London dry gin
Two dashes of sweet gomme syrup
Chilled dry champagne
A twist of lemon

◆ In a champagne flute or cocktail glass, pour a measure of gin and add the two dashes of gomme syrup.
◆ Top up with champagne.
◆ Garnish with the twist of lemon.

THE WEDDING BELLE

A pretty cocktail with which to toast the bride.

Crushed ice

One part gin

One part Dubonnet rouge

Half a part cherry brandy

One part fresh orange juice

◈ Place two tablespoons of crushed ice in a
   cocktail shaker, add the gin, Dubonnet, cherry
   brandy and orange juice and shake well.
◈ Strain into a cocktail glass and serve.

THE CHIHUAHUA BITE

Like the famous miniature Mexican dog, this
drink may be petite but it certainly is lively.

Ice cubes

Three parts London dry gin

One part Calvados

One part lime juice cordial

A twist of lemon rind

◈ Place three ice cubes in a cocktail shaker and
   add the gin, Calvados and lime juice cordial.
◈ Shake well and strain into a cocktail glass.
◈ Twist the lemon rind over it and drop it into
   the glass as garnish.

The Wedding Belle (right front) *was originally
made to toast a pretty bride. The Chihuahua Bite
(right back)* is an aptly named, fierce little drink.

RUM

Rum is a rich and fragrant spirit distilled from molasses in a pot still or patent still. Because sugar cane is usually grown in tropical climates, and molasses is produced from sugar cane, the drink has become associated with the tropics, sun-drenched islands and white beaches edged with waving palm trees.

As with most distilled spirits, rum is clear when it comes from the still, but is matured in oak casks and often coloured with caramel before bottling. Jamaican rum is usually dark, Cuban comes in light, gold or dark, while Puerto Rican rum is left clear. A smooth and velvety rum is made in the Dominican Republic and some fine rums are produced in Haiti, Barbados, Antigua, Trinidad and Venezuela.

For many years rum formed part of the rations of sailors in the British Royal Navy. Their Pussers Rum (derived from the word "purser") was made in the British Virgin Islands and was issued as standard navy ration for three centuries. When particularly dangerous jobs had to be done, the men were sometimes given an extra ration of rum to give them the necessary courage.

In a really rough storm one of the worst things that could happen was that the brace controlling the mainsail yard would break under stress. Sailors would then have to go aloft in gale conditions, secure the two flogging ends of the broken mainbrace and go about the tricky task of splicing the ends together. One slip and they could crash down onto the heaving deck or, worse, be flung overboard into the foaming sea to be lost forever.

This hazardous task called for a stiff draught of courage and gave rise to the expression: "Splice the mainbrace."

Drinkers have discovered that the rich rum taste combines perfectly with fruit juice to give a tropical flavour to cocktails, and there are hundreds of rum-based cocktail recipes available to enthusiastic mixologists.

BRASS MONKEY

The "brass monkey" in the name was the brass rack on which cannon balls were stored in the days of sailing ship warfare.

In very cold weather the brass would contract and sometimes the cannon balls would no longer fit on the shrunken monkey and would pop out, causing some confusion as they rolled about on the gun deck.

Hence the expression: "Cold enough to freeze the balls off a brass monkey."

The cocktail is a good warmer when the temperature reaches brass monkey levels.

Ice cubes
One part light rum
One part vodka
Four parts orange juice
A slice of orange

- Fill a highball glass with ice cubes and pour the rum, vodka and orange juice over them.
- Stir carefully and serve decorated with the slice of orange and a pretty straw.

"A man shouldn't fool with booze until he is fifty. Then he's a damn fool if he doesn't."

William Faulkner

DAIQUIRI

Man is a creative animal and has been shown to adapt to almost any circumstances.

American engineers working in Daiquiri, Cuba, were upset to discover they could not obtain their usual drink, bourbon, there. But there was rum in plentiful supply, so they set about creating a drink to replace their favourite tipple.

The daiquiri was born. As with most famous cocktails, there are many versions of the daiquiri, but this simple one should serve as a starting point for the creative cocktail artist.

Ice cubes
One part light rum (traditionally Cuban, of course)
The juice of half a lime
Half a teaspoon of sugar
A slice of lime
A cocktail cherry

* Place four or five ice cubes in a cocktail shaker. Add the rum, lime juice and sugar.
* Shake very thoroughly, then strain it into a cocktail glass.
* Decorate with a slice of lime and the cocktail cherry spiked on a stick.

Ernest Hemingway always ordered double Daiquiris (right) when he frequented La Floradita Bar in Havana, Cuba. The Brass Monkey (far right) has nothing to do with primates but originated, not surprisingly, in the navy.

DAIQUIRI BLOSSOM

Not everybody enjoys the sharp astringency of the daiquiri described on the previous page. Maybe it was fine for homesick mining engineers, but in the comfort of your own home or a cosy cocktail bar you may prefer this sweeter version. It certainly has a tropical flavour to it.

The Daiquiri, like the Martini, comes in many guises – Banana Daiquiri (above left), Daiquiri Blossom (above centre) and Frozen Pineapple Daiquiri (above right).

Ice cubes

One part light rum

One part freshly squeezed orange juice

A dash of maraschino

A slice of orange

A cocktail cherry

◆ Place four or five ice cubes in a cocktail shaker. Add the rum, orange juice and dash of maraschino.

◆ Shake well and strain into a cocktail glass.

◆ Decorate with the slice of orange and the cherry speared together on a cocktail stick.

BANANA DAIQUIRI

In his popular Discworld novels, author Terry Pratchett writes about an orang-utan who is inordinately fond of banana daiquiris. Readers all over the world send Pratchett recipes for this now-famous drink. This one is from a South African fan.

Two parts light rum
One part banana liqueur
One part fresh lime juice
Half a medium-sized banana
Crushed ice
A slice of kiwi fruit, if available

- Place the rum, liqueur, lime juice and banana in a blender and blend for about 10 seconds until smooth and creamy.
- Add two generous scoops of crushed ice and blend for a further second or two, just to chill the drink.
- Strain it into a goblet, garnish it with the slice of kiwi fruit (or you could use a slice of banana in an emergency) and serve with a straw.

Billie Dove and Paul Lukas gaze intently into one another's eyes in The Night Watch *(right).*

FROZEN PINEAPPLE DAIQUIRI

Of course, you can go all the way with the tropical drink theme and make this rather exotic version of the famous drink. Looks good, tastes great!

One part light rum (naturally)
Juice of half a lime
Two teaspoons of Cointreau
Two slices of ripe pineapple, cut into cubes
Crushed ice
A cocktail cherry

- Place the rum, lime juice, Cointreau and pineapple cubes in a blender and give them a whizz until the mixture is smooth and frothy.
- Half-fill a champagne flute with crushed ice and pour the mixture over it.
- Decorate with a final cube of pineapple and the cherry spiked together on a cocktail stick.

THE BEE'S KISS

It's not hard to guess how this sweet delight got
its name. As with any bee, however, too much
familiarity could produce a sting.

Crushed ice
Two parts light rum
One part clear honey
One part thick cream

◈ Place about a cup of crushed ice in a cocktail
   shaker and pour the rum, honey and cream
   over it.
◈ Shake vigorously until well blended.
◈ Strain into a chilled cocktail glass and
   serve ungarnished.

*Between the sheets is a drink to be shared
with a very close friend.*

*The Bee's Kiss is one of remarkably few
cocktails to specify honey as an ingredient.*

BETWEEN THE SHEETS

The perfect end to a long day is to slip in
between the sheets – crisp, clean and comforting.
Perhaps the inventor of this cocktail felt all those
attributes had been captured in the glass.

Ice cubes
One part light rum
One part brandy
One part Cointreau
A teaspoon of lemon juice
A twist of lemon rind

◈ Place five or six ice cubes in a cocktail
   shaker. Add the rum, brandy, Cointreau
   and lemon juice.
◈ Shake well and strain into a cocktail glass.
◈ Serve garnished with a twist of lemon rind.

HENRY MORGAN'S GROG

Grog was the name given to the mixture of equal parts of rum and water served to sailors in the British Royal Navy (as decreed by a naval officer nicknamed "Old Grog" after the grogram jackets he liked to wear at sea). Captain Morgan's version of grog is rather different and far more powerful.

Crushed ice
One part dark Jamaican rum
Two parts Pernod
Two parts whisky
One part thick cream
Ground nutmeg

❋ Place a scoop of crushed ice in a blender or cocktail shaker and add the rum, Pernod, whisky and cream.
❋ Blend or shake briskly until well mixed, and then strain it into a lowball glass.
❋ Dust ground nutmeg over it before serving.

APRICOT PIE

This is a fresh little cocktail for summer drinking. It's tangy and fruity and absolutely guaranteed to have you coming back for more.

Crushed ice
One part light rum
One part sweet vermouth
One teaspoon apricot brandy or to taste
One teaspoon fresh lemon juice or to taste
One teaspoon grenadine or to taste
Orange peel to garnish

❋ Place a generous scoop of crushed ice in a cocktail shaker or a blender and add the rum, sweet vermouth, apricot brandy, lemon juice and grenadine.
❋ Shake or blend well and strain into a chilled cocktail glass.
❋ Twist the orange peel over the drink to release the zest, then drop it in as decoration.

Henry Morgan's Grog (right) *is a pirate version of grog, the Royal Navy's drink comprising equal quantities of rum and water.*

TOM AND JERRY

This classic cocktail is not actually named after the famous cartoon cat and mouse duo. It was invented way back in the 1850s by one Jerry Thomas, called "the professor", in his famous Planter's House bar in St Louis, Missouri. Later the name just naturally changed from Jerry Thomas to Tom and Jerry.

One egg
Half a part sugar syrup (or less to taste)
One part dark Jamaican rum
One part cognac
Boiling water
Grated nutmeg

◆ Separate the yolk of the egg from the white and beat each separately. Fold them together and add the sugar syrup.
◆ Place this mixture in a warmed coffee mug, add the rum and cognac and top up with boiling water.
◆ Sprinkle grated nutmeg on top and serve piping hot.

THE ZOMBIE

A zombie is a corpse that has been brought back to life. Maybe the name of this cocktail refers to its restorative powers.

Ice cubes
One part dark rum
One part light rum
One part apricot brandy
One part fresh pineapple juice
A squeeze of lemon juice
A squeeze of orange juice
A slice of pineapple

◆ Place four ice cubes in a cocktail shaker and add the dark and light rum, brandy, pineapple juice and the two squeezes of citrus juice.
◆ Shake well and strain into a wine goblet.
◆ Garnish with a slice of pineapple and a cherry threaded together on a cocktail stick.

"It's no time for mirth and laughter,
The cold grey dawn of the
morning after."

George Ade

The Zombie (above front) *and Tom and Jerry* (above back) *are two rum-based cocktails reputed to cure the common cold – or two ways to help you forget its misery!*

CUBA LIBRE

This classic cocktail is reputed to have been invented by an army officer in Cuba shortly after Coca-Cola was first produced back in the 1890s.

Crushed ice
One generous part light rum
The juice of a lime
Cola
A slice of lime

◆ In a highball glass, place a small scoop of crushed ice and pour in the rum and lime juice.
◆ Top up with Cola and garnish with a thin wedge of fresh lime.
◆ It is usually served with a swizzle stick or stirrer.

Cuba Libre (right) is one of the most famous of all rum-based drinks and has been immortalised in the old Calypso song, "Rum and Coca-Cola".

THE DEVIL'S TAIL

Only the very brave can catch the devil by his tail, but those who do are safe from his horns. This is definitely a drink for the bold in spirit.

Crushed ice
Three parts light rum
One part vodka
One part apricot liqueur
One part lime juice
A dash of grenadine
Lime peel

◆ Place a scoop of crushed ice in a shaker or blender and add the rum, vodka, apricot liqueur, lime juice (preferably fresh) and grenadine.
◆ Shake or blend well and strain into a lowball glass.
◆ Twist the lime peel over the glass and drop it into the drink.

Betty Compson pours John Darrow a restorative drink in The Lady Refuses.

THE TALL ISLANDER

The name refers to the length of the drink, rather than its creator. It's long and cooling and has a distinctly tropical flavour.

Ice cubes

One part light rum

A dash of dark Jamaican rum

One part pineapple juice

A dash of lime juice

One teaspoon of sugar syrup

Chilled soda water

A slice of lime

◆ Place four ice cubes in a cocktail shaker and add the light and dark rum, pineapple juice, lime juice and sugar syrup.

◆ Shake well and strain into a highball glass.

◆ Add a splash of soda water and several ice cubes.

◆ Garnish with the slice of lime.

"The only cure for a real **hangover** is death."

Robert Benchley

HOT BUTTERED RUM

No collection of rum drinks would be complete without at least one recipe for hot buttered rum. It's a warm, sustaining drink to serve on a freezing winter's night by a roaring log fire. Buttered rum is mentioned by Charles Dickens in his book *Hard Times*. "Take a glass of scalding rum and butter before you get into bed," Bounderby says to Mrs Sparsit.

The peel of a lemon or orange
Whole cloves
One tablespoon of brown sugar
A cinnamon stick
A liberal helping of dark Jamaican rum
Half as much crème de cacao
A pat of unsalted butter
Grated nutmeg

◈ Warm a large coffee mug by filling it with boiling water and letting it stand for a minute. While it is warming, take the citrus peel and stud it with as many whole cloves as you can.

◈ Empty the coffee mug and place the studded peel in it, together with the brown sugar and cinnamon stick. Add a little boiling water and stir until the sugar has dissolved.

◈ Now add the rum and crème de cacao and fill the mug with hot water.

◈ Remove the cinnamon stick. Drop in the butter, stir and sprinkle with grated nutmeg.

The Devil's Tail (above front) is a fiery little drink that could well be served as a "tail end" to an evening meal.
In parts of Britian and America Hot Buttered Rum (above back) is as popular as Glühwein or the Tom and Jerry as a winter tradition.

El Burro is heavily loaded with all sorts of flavours and probably gets its name (the donkey) from the fact that it has quite a kick to it.

EL BURRO

This delightful drink should be drunk in moderation if you don't want to make an ass of yourself!

Crushed ice
One part Kahlua
One and a half parts dark rum
One and a half parts coconut cream
Two parts thin cream

Half a banana
Sprig of fresh mint
Slices of banana

- Place two spoonfuls of crushed ice in a blender and add all the other ingredients, except the mint and the slices of banana.
- Blend at high speed for about 10 seconds.
- Strain into a large goblet and garnish with the slices of banana and sprig of mint.

No matter where it is made, rum is traditionally associated with tropical islands, the Caribbean and sailing ships. This is reflected in the label of the French Rhum Vieux (above). Norma Shearer (opposite) as the happy divorcee in The Divorcee.

THE FLUFFY DUCK

It's interesting how many of the cocktails containing cream are named after animals or birds. We have the burro, the pink squirrel and the grasshopper. Now meet the duck.

One part light rum

One part advocaat

Lemonade

Half a part thin cream

A fresh strawberry and a sprig of mint

◈ Pour the Bacardi and advocaat into a highball glass and fill almost to the top with well-chilled lemonade.

◈ Trickle the cream onto the surface over the back of a spoon and garnish with the strawberry and sprig of mint.

The Fluffy Duck – a sophisticated concoction of rum, advocaat and lemonade.

Unlike the recipes for most other cocktails in this book, the "parts" used in the Zombie Punch should be half-litre jugs rather than dinky little bar measures.

ZOMBIE PUNCH

There is something a little mysterious about the idea of a zombie, and this drink certainly has a murky and mysterious look to match its name. The flavour, however, is full of life.

Two parts light Puerto Rican rum

One part dark Jamaican rum

One part dark Demerara rum

One part Triple Sec

One part fresh lime juice

One part fresh orange juice

A quarter part lemon juice

A quarter part papaya juice

A quarter part pineapple juice

A splash of Pernod

A large chunk of ice

Pineapple slices

- Mix all the liquid ingredients together in a large punch bowl, place the ice in the centre and allow it to stand for a few hours to chill.
- Before the guests arrive, taste it and adjust the flavour by adding the appropriate fruit juices or spirits.
- Garnish with slices of pineapple shortly before serving.

XALAPA PUNCH

This cocktail probably originated from Xalapa, a cathedral town situated in the province of Vera Cruz in Mexico.

Here again, the size of your measure will be determined by the size of your punch bowl. In these informal times almost any large bowl will do. I have even seen punch served in a brass-bound wooden bucket. It looked great!

The zest of two large oranges, grated

Two parts strong black tea

Honey or sugar to taste (about a cupful)

One part golden rum

One part Calvados

One part red wine

A block of ice

Orange and lemon slices

- Place the grated orange zest in a saucepan and pour the hot tea over it to absorb the flavour. Leave it to cool and add the honey or sugar. Stir until dissolved.
- Add the rum, Calvados and red wine and place in the fridge to chill.
- When ready to serve, place the block of ice in the punch bowl, pour the punch over it and garnish it with slices of orange and lemon.

"And when the ball was over
Everyone confessed
They all enjoyed the DANCING
But the DRINKING was the best."

Anon

VODKA

The word "vodka" comes from the Russian "Zhiznennia voda" which means "water of life". Vodka, or wodka, means "little water".

Vodka is pure spirit and can be distilled from a number of sources, including potatoes and sugar cane. The spirit is then filtered through charcoal to remove any oils or traces of impurities, and the resultant liquor is the perfect base for a cocktail. It adds the kick of alcohol without doing much to alter the flavour of the drink. Add vodka to lemonade and, voilà! you have alcoholic lemonade. It's as simple as that.

Vodka became popular in America in about 1946, when wartime rationing had created all kinds of shortages and drinkers grabbed whatever was available. Smirnoff vodka had been around as a rather unusual drink for some time, but nobody took it seriously until it was all they could get. It didn't take long to gather a loyal following.

One of the selling points of vodka is that it is almost odourless, so it cannot be detected on your breath.

Vodka is the ideal drink for the beginner bartender to use in experiments. Whatever new flavour of mixer comes onto the market, from chocolate mint cream to carrot and pumpkin juice, you just add vodka and you've invented a new cocktail.

Typical of the popular vodka-based drinks is the Screwdriver, which consists of vodka and orange juice and is said to have been invented by construction workers who wanted to add excitement to their lunchtime drink of orange juice. A dash of vodka made the difference, and a quick stir with a handy screwdriver got it properly mixed into the juice.

Ideally, vodka should be stored in the freezer and served almost painfully cold. Purists like to drink it neat, tossing back a small glass in a single gulp.

VODKATINI

It's interesting to see what factors influence the popularity of a cocktail. The vodka martini must be one of the best-known cocktails in the world today, just because the famous and fictitious James Bond, 007, has been drinking vodka martinis for the past 36 years.

Ice cubes
Two parts vodka (preferably from Russia)
One part dry vermouth
A twist of lemon rind

◆ Place about five ice cubes in a bar glass, add the vodka and vermouth and stir well.
◆ Strain the mixture into a cocktail glass and decorate it with a twist of lemon rind.

Immortalised by Ian Fleming's James Bond, the Vodkatini is simply a martini made with vodka instead of gin.

Another vodka-based cocktail, the Q Martini (above left) has the added attraction of being blue. Legend has it that the barman of Harry's New York Bar in Paris named the Bloody Mary (above right) after the glamorous Hollywood actress, Mary Pickford.

THE Q MARTINI

The James Bond series of books and films has spawned a number of popular drinks, including this intriguing blue version of the Martini.

Ice cubes

Two parts vodka

A splash of blue Curaçao

Half a part lime juice

A twist of lemon rind

- Place three ice cubes in a cocktail bar glass. Add the vodka, blue Curaçao and lime juice.
- Stir until well blended and strain into a cocktail glass.
- Decorate with a twist of lemon rind.

BLOODY MARY

Today the Bloody Mary is probably the most popular vodka-based cocktail in the world and there are many variations of this tempting drink.

But it must have taken some courage to create the first one. It needs imagination to blend two such disparate drinks as fiery, crystal-clear vodka and thick, slightly lumpy tomato juice. But there's no doubt it works, whatever way you make it. Here's a starter recipe.

Ice cubes

Two parts vodka

Six parts tomato juice

A teaspoon of tomato sauce (catsup)

A dash of Worcestershire sauce

A dash of Tabasco sauce

A pinch of celery salt

A stick of celery

A dusting of ground white pepper

- Place four ice cubes in a cocktail shaker and add the vodka and tomato juice.
- Add the tomato sauce, Worcestershire sauce, Tabasco sauce and celery salt.
- Shake well and strain into a highball glass.
- Serve decorated with a stick of celery.
- Finish with a light dusting of white pepper. (You could use black pepper, but it looks very unappetising, rather like cigar ash on the surface of the drink.)

The ingredients for Russian Coffee (above) and the White Russian (page 90) are similar. The difference is in the colour of the coffee liqueur used.

RUSSIAN COFFEE

The Russians have the reputation not only of making the best vodka but of being able to drink it in large quantities. And who needs ordinary coffee when there's a drink as warming as this one to keep out the Siberian chill? Names and styles vary from bartender to bartender.

One part vodka
One part coffee liqueur (Tia Maria or Kahlua)
One part thin cream
Half a cup of crushed ice
Cocoa powder (optional)

◆ Place all the ingredients in a blender and give them a brisk whirl for about 10 seconds.
◆ Pour the result into a chilled champagne saucer and decorate with a swirl of cream.
◆ You could also sprinkle a dusting of cocoa powder on the surface for added flavour.

"A woman drove me to drink

and I didn't even have the courtesy

to thank her."

W. C. Fields

BLACK COSSACK

Why anybody should want to mess with
Guinness, goodness knows. But this is a simple
drink and popular in some parts.

A large slug of vodka
A glass of Guinness stout

◈ Simply pour the vodka carefully into the
stout and drink it. Don't stir or shake it, as
the froth would be overwhelming.

BLUE LAGOON

The Blue Lagoon is a cooling, ice blue summer
drink. There's always something a little special
about serving a blue drink.

Crushed ice
Three parts vodka
One part blue Curaçao
Three parts pineapple juice
Three dashes of green chartreuse
A slice of pineapple
A cocktail cherry (optional)

◈ Place half a cup of crushed ice in a cocktail
shaker and add the vodka, Curaçao, pineapple
juice and green chartreuse.
◈ Shake well and strain into a lowball glass.
◈ Serve decorated with a slice of pineapple, and
a cocktail cherry if you feel like adding even
more colour.

*Add a touch of mystery to a cocktail party
with a Blue Lagoon (above left). The Black
Cossack (above right) is a stunningly simple
combination of vodka and Guinness.*

Bullshot is an unusual drink reputed to be a quick cure for a hangover.

BULLSHOT

We should not be surprised to find vodka teamed up with savoury flavours after the great success of the Bloody Mary. The Bullshot is reputed to be a fine remedy for hangover blues.

Ice cubes

One part vodka

Three parts chilled clear beef bouillon

A dash of lemon juice

A dash of Worcestershire sauce

A pinch of celery salt

A slice of lemon

◆ Place five or six ice cubes in a bar glass and add the vodka and beef bouillon.

◆ Add the lemon juice, Worcestershire sauce and celery salt.

◆ Stir well and strain over ice cubes in a lowball glass.

◆ Serve garnished with a lemon slice.

Robert Montgomery (opposite) *raises his glass in* Letty Lynton.

HARVEY WALLBANGER

The story behind the intriguing name of this drink is that Harvey was a surfer who was eliminated in a surfing championship in California. He was so angry at his defeat that he headed for Pancho's Bar at Manhattan Beach and soothed his bruised ego by drinking a large quantity of vodka and Galliano. He then banged his head against a wall and urged his friends to take him home and stop his destructive drinking.

Whether it's true or not, the name has stuck and the drink is a firm favourite throughout the world.

Ice cubes

Two parts vodka

Five parts fresh orange juice

One part Galliano

A slice of orange

◆ Place four or five ice cubes in a cocktail shaker and add the vodka and orange juice.

◆ Shake well and strain into a highball glass.

◆ Add two ice cubes and gently float the Galliano on top.

◆ Garnish with a slice of orange on the rim of the glass and serve with a straw.

The Harvey Wallbanger (left) – a frustrated surfer's gift to the world of cocktails.

- Place two ice cubes in a chilled highball glass and pour in the vodka and lime juice.
- Stir well and fill with ginger beer.
- Garnish with the lime and serve.

THE VOLGA BOATMAN

I doubt whether any Volga boatman could have afforded this delightful drink, unless his boat happened to be an elegant pleasure craft, but it's a pleasantly cheerful drink.

Crushed ice
One part vodka
One part cherry brandy
One part fresh orange juice
A maraschino cherry

- Place three spoons of crushed ice in a cocktail shaker and add the vodka, cherry brandy and orange juice.
- Shake well and strain into a cocktail glass.
- Garnish with the cherry on a cocktail stick and serve.

The Moscow Mule (above left) *and The Volga Boatman* (above right) *demonstrate how vodka teams up with any fruit flavours.*

MOSCOW MULE

You can now buy ready-mixed Moscow Mules in cans, but it's far more fun to make your own, complete with your own variations and personal touches. When it comes to cocktails, creativity is the name of the game.

Ice cubes
One generous part vodka
A teaspoon of lime juice
Ginger beer
A slice of fresh lime

"You're not drunk

if you can lie on the floor

without holding on."

Dean Martin

WHITE RUSSIAN

This smooth white cocktail probably reminded its inventor of the glistening snow of Siberia. It's certainly a great comforter on a frosty night.

Crushed ice
One part vodka
One part white crème de cacao
One part thick cream

◈ Place two spoons of crushed ice in a cocktail shaker and add the vodka, crème de cacao and cream.
◈ Shake well and strain into a chilled cocktail glass and serve ungarnished.

BANANA PUNCH

Here's a truly tropical drink which uses three kinds of fruit flavours to create a jungle taste.

Crushed ice
One part vodka
One part apricot brandy
The juice of half a lime
Soda water
A sliced banana
A sprig of fresh mint

◈ Place a scoop of crushed ice in a cocktail shaker and add the vodka, apricot brandy and lime juice.
◈ Shake well and strain into a highball glass.
◈ Top up with soda water and decorate with slices of banana and the mint.

The White Russian (above left), a rich and creamy drink for a chilly evening, and Banana punch (above right), one of those deliciously dangerous drinks that will last you the whole evening.

VODKA GIMLET

We often encounter the vodka equivalents of
drinks that were originally made with gin. This is
a typical one and, like the original Gimlet, there
are many versions of this classic drink. We offer a
basic version and leave it to you to create your
own personal variations.

Ice cubes

Two parts vodka

One part Rose's lime juice cordial

A teaspoon of sugar syrup

A slice of orange

* Place three ice cubes in a cocktail shaker and
  add the vodka, lime juice and sugar syrup.
* Shake well and strain into a cocktail glass.
* Garnish with a slice of orange.

SALVATORE

This is one of those superb cocktails that
manages to combine sweet and tart flavours in
exactly the right proportions (as long as you do it
right, of course).

Ice cubes

Two parts vodka

One part Kirsch

One part Cointreau

One part fresh grapefruit juice

A maraschino cherry

* Place four ice cubes in a cocktail shaker
  and add the vodka, Kirsch, Cointreau and
  grapefruit juice.
* Shake well and strain into a cocktail glass.
* Serve decorated with a cherry on a
  cocktail stick.

*Sweet and sour flavours combine happily
in the Vodka Gimlet (above left) and the
tangy Salvatore (above right).*

SCOTCH FROG

I have no idea how this rather punchy drink got its name. Perhaps it is rather like Welsh rarebit, which is reputed to be the poor Welsh householder's substitute for rabbit. But why should any self-respecting Scot want a substitute for a frog?

Ice cubes
Two parts vodka
One part Galliano
One part Cointreau
The juice of a lime
A dash of Angostura bitters
Maraschino cherry juice or cherry liqueur

◆ Place three ice cubes in a cocktail shaker and add the vodka, Galliano, Cointreau, lime juice, bitters and cherry juice or cherry liqueur.
◆ Shake well and strain into a cocktail glass.
◆ Serve ungarnished.

"I fear the man who drinks water, as he remembers this morning what the rest of us said last night."

Greek saying

The Absolut bottle (left) is made of special translucent glass and the label is engraved rather than stuck on the bottle.

THE BLACK MARBLE

Like many of the great classics of the cocktail world, the Black Marble is uncomplicated, but very chic.

Ice cubes
A large black olive
One part good Polish or Russian vodka
A slice of orange

◆ Fill a lowball glass or wine goblet with ice cubes. Place the black olive right in the centre and pour the vodka over it.
◆ Serve garnished with a slice of fresh orange.

The Black Marble (above front) *has the elegant simplicity of a good dry martini. The tartness of lime is offset by the sweetness of the liqueurs in the Scotch Frog* (above rear).

Cherry vodka (above left) is a pretty little drink that looks deceptively innocent but should be handled with respect. The Kremlin Colonel (above right) ranks high in the vodka cocktail hierarchy.

CHERRY VODKA

Vodka combines well with almost any fruit flavour, as this pretty cocktail demonstrates.

Crushed ice
Two parts chilled vodka
One part fresh lime juice
One part cherry liqueur
A maraschino cherry

- Place three spoons of crushed ice in a cocktail shaker, add the vodka, lime juice and cherry liqueur and shake well.
- Strain into a chilled cocktail glass.
- Decorate with the cherry on a cocktail stick.

THE KREMLIN COLONEL

This simple vodka-based creation was considered good enough for promotion to the highest rank.

Crushed ice
Two parts vodka
Half a part fresh lime juice
A teaspoon of sugar (or to taste)
Mint leaves

- Place a spoon of ice in a cocktail shaker and add the vodka, lime juice and sugar.
- Shake well and strain into a cocktail glass.
- Tear the mint leaves to release the aroma and drop them on to the drink as garnish.

Undoubtedly Russian in origin and style, the Soviet (above left) is a punchy little drink. The Salty Dog (above right) is almost a classic and is to vodka what margarita is to tequila.

THE SOVIET

Like the cuddly Russian bear, this vodka drink is stronger than it looks.

Crushed ice

Three parts vodka

One part sweet sherry

One part dry vermouth

Lemon peel

- Place a scoop of crushed ice in a shaker, add the vodka, sherry and vermouth and shake well.
- Strain into a cocktail glass and serve garnished with the lemon peel.

SALTY DOG

The salted rim of the glass used for this cocktail turns it into a complete taste experience.

Ice cubes

Four parts vodka

One part unsweetened grapefruit juice

One teaspoon lemon juice

Salt

- Place three ice cubes in a cocktail shaker and add the vodka, grapefruit juice and lemon juice and shake well.
- Frost the rim of a chilled cocktail glass with fine salt and strain the cocktail into glass.

WHISKY

Whisky (or whiskey, depending on its origin) is made in many parts of the world. The spirit produced in Scotland is probably the best known and is spelled without the "e", whisky. This is usually simply referred to as Scotch. All other whiskies are spelled with an "e" to distinguish them from the "real thing".

It should be said right away that most Scots would be horrified at the thought of their national drink being adulterated with anything at all, apart from a little water to bring out the natural flavour. Unless you are an active masochist it is not advisable to offer a whisky-based cocktail to a true Scot.

This is probably why almost all whisky and whiskey cocktails were developed in America and not Scotland. This being so, the chances are the original recipes calling for "whisky" referred to American bourbon and not Scotch.

Good whisky is also made in Ireland, Canada and even in Japan, so there are many different flavours from which to choose.

Even in Scotland there are many styles of whisky that come from the various producing areas. Some of the best known are "single malts", which are produced from a particular distillery, while most commercially available whiskies are blended ones, made from the products of several regions.

Essentially, whisky is distilled from a fermented mash made of malted grain. In Scotland it derives much of its rich flavour from peat. The water used in whisky-making flows over peat beds, picking up its earthy flavour, and peat is burned to warm the sprouted grain and stop further growth. The pale blue smoke leaves its distinctive flavour in the malt.

SCOTCH OLD-FASHIONED

Here's a cocktail that adds a bittersweet touch to whisky. No doubt the Scots would disapprove strongly of any addition to what they believe is already the perfect drink, but if you're not Scottish you might like to try it.

A cube of sugar
A few dashes of Angostura bitters
Two measures of Scotch whisky
Ice cubes

◆ Soak a sugar cube in Angostura bitters and place it in the bottom of a lowball glass.
◆ Add just enough water to dissolve the sugar and then pour in the measures of whisky. Stir gently and drop in two ice cubes.

THREE RIVERS

Invented in Canada and often known by its French name, Trois Rivieres, this drink has become an international classic.

Ice cubes
Two parts whiskey
  (preferably Canadian)
One part Dubonnet
One part Triple Sec

◆ Place four or five ice cubes in a cocktail shaker and add the whiskey, Dubonnet and Triple Sec.
◆ Shake well and strain into a lowball glass.
◆ Serve ungarnished.

MINT JULEP

This drink reeks of good living in an age when there were slaves and servants available at the flick of a finger to do the bidding of the master.

A good Mint Julep is a drink for the wealthy. Not many people today will be able to afford the "tankard of bourbon" that forms the basis of the drink. But for those occasions when you do feel like a millionaire, here's the recipe.

Crushed ice
A tankard of bourbon
A teaspoon of caster sugar
Two tablespoons of water
A teaspoon of Barbados rum
A large bunch of freshly picked mint

◆ Place a cup of crushed ice in a pitcher and add the bourbon, caster sugar, water and rum. Stir well.

◆ Crush the mint leaves lightly to release the flavour and place them in a serving jug.

◆ Strain the contents of the bar glass into the jug, add four or five ice cubes and serve in lowball glasses.

Clockwise from top: Mint Julep originated in the United States' Deep South in the days of the cotton barons and Mississippi steamboats. The Scotch Old-Fashioned, a classic cocktail, was created around 1900. Although probably first made with Canadian whiskey, Three Rivers tastes just as good made with any good whisky.

ROB ROY

This drink, named after the famous Scottish
hero, should be poured whenever a toast is drunk
to heroes.

Ice cubes

Two dashes of Angostura bitters

One generous part Scotch whisky

One equally generous part sweet vermouth

A twist of orange

◈ Place two ice cubes in a lowball glass and
   splash in two dashes of bitters.

◈ Add the whisky and vermouth, garnish with
   a twist of orange and serve.

*The Waldorf Cocktail is traditionally made with
bourbon rather than Scotch whisky.*

*Experts say this is absolutely the only drink to
enjoy on St Andrew's Day. The Rob Roy should
be made only with real Scotch.*

THE WALDORF COCKTAIL

By using different blends of whisky you can
create a whole range of different Waldorf
cocktails. Traditionally, bourbon is used.

Crushed ice

Two parts bourbon

One part Pernod

One part sweet vermouth

A dash of Angostura bitters

◈ Place a scoop of crushed ice in a bar glass and
   add the bourbon, Pernod, sweet vermouth and
   Angostura bitters.

◈ Stir well, strain into a chilled cocktail glass.

LADY HUNT

An elegant and delicious cocktail that is tangy and crisp in character, but also gently mellow.

Three parts malt whisky

One part Tia Maria

One part Amaretto

The juice of half a lemon

A dash of egg white

Ice cubes

A slice of orange

A maraschino cherry

◈ Place all the ingredients with the exception of the orange slice and cherry into a cocktail shaker with four ice cubes and shake briskly.

◈ Strain into a cocktail glass and decorate with the slice of orange and the maraschino cherry.

The original version of the Lady Hunt was created by Salvatore Calabrese, one of Britain's best-known bartenders, specially for Lady Caroline Hunt, the founder of Rosewood Hotels.

New Orleans (above left) is a tangy and complex array of flavours. In Spirit of Scotland (above right), two well-known products of Scotland are combined.

SPIRIT OF SCOTLAND

Most appropriately named, as Drambuie is made of whisky, heather and honey. What could be more Scottish?

Crushed ice

Two parts Scotch whisky

One part Drambuie

Half a part lemon juice

◆ Place a scoop of crushed ice in a blender or cocktail shaker and add the whisky, Drambuie and lemon juice.

◆ Blend everything together briskly and strain into a cocktail glass.

"Freedom and **whisky** gang the gither!"

Robert Burns

NEW ORLEANS

Many cocktails got their names from the places where they were invented. This one obviously originated in the southern United States and evokes images of the Mardi Gras and Dixieland jazz.

Crushed ice

Three parts bourbon

One part Pernod

Three dashes of Angostura bitters

A dash of anisette

A teaspoon of sugar syrup (or less to taste)

Ice cubes

A twist of lemon

◆ Place a scoop of crushed ice in a cocktail shaker and add the bourbon, Pernod, bitters, anisette and sugar syrup.

◆ Shake vigorously and strain into a lowball glass filled with ice cubes. Garnish with a twist of lemon before serving.

Although Scots purists insist that whisky should be taken neat, this malt-based spirit (opposite) has found a permanent place in the cocktail bar and is the base for many delicious drinks.

The Leprechaun is a merry little Irish drink which calls for a good measure of fine Irish whiskey.

SAZERAC

This romantic drink derived its name from the company importing brandy from France, Sazerac du Forge et Fils. Later, rye whiskey replaced the brandy in the recipe, but the name remained the same.

A lump of sugar
A dash of Angostura bitters
Ice cubes
Two generous parts rye whiskey
A dash of Pernod
A twist of lemon

- Soak the sugar lump in Angostura bitters and place it in a cooled lowball glass with an ice cube.
- Add the whiskey and stir well. Add the Pernod and twist the lemon rind over the glass.

LEPRECHAUN

It is said that if you capture a leprechaun he will grant you a wish, but who could wish for more than this merry wee drink?

Ice cubes
One part Irish whiskey (a large one, of course)
Two parts tonic water
Lemon peel

- Place two ice cubes in a highball glass and add the whiskey and tonic.
- Stir reverently and twist the lemon peel over it. Drop in the twisted peel and serve.

"Love makes the world go round. Whisky makes it go round twice as fast."

Compton Mackenzie

SCOTCH MIST

The simplest version of Scotch Mist is simply Scotch on the rocks with a twist of lemon zest over it. This hot version is served in a tea cup and is known, for some strange reason, as the "English" Scotch mist. It's probably something to do with the tea.

This version of Scotch Mist (below left) is served hot. The Sazerac (below right) is a romantic drink that originated in New Orleans.

One part Scotch whisky

Three parts freshly brewed
  Ceylon tea

Honey

Thick cream

- Mix the whisky and tea together and add the honey to taste, stirring over a low heat until almost (but not quite) boiling.
- Pour into small (demitasse) coffee cups and float a teaspoon of cream onto the surface of each drink.

COMFORTABLE SCREW

Southern Comfort is a delicious orange-and-peach-flavoured whiskey produced in the southern United States.

Ice cubes
One part Southern Comfort
Six parts fresh orange juice
A banana

◆ Place six ice cubes in a cocktail shaker and add the Southern Comfort and orange juice.
◆ Shake well and strain into a lowball glass.
◆ Garnish with the banana and serve.

CLUBMAN COCKTAIL

Irish Mist is a liqueur based on Irish whiskey flavoured with herbs and honey and produced in Tulach Mhor, Ireland. The Clubman is a very colourful drink, guaranteed to start the conversation flowing.

Ice cubes
One part Irish Mist
Four parts orange juice
A dessertspoon of egg white
A dash of blue Curaçao

◆ Place four ice cubes in a cocktail shaker and add the Irish Mist, orange juice and egg white.
◆ Shake briskly and strain into a lowball glass.
◆ Carefully trickle the blue Curaçao down the sides of the glass (you might like to use a straw) to create a marbled effect.

The Comfortable Screw (far left) gets its rather naughty name from the fact that it is a Screwdriver made with Southern Comfort instead of vodka. In the Clubman Cocktail (left), blue Curaçao is trickled down the sides of the glass to create the blue veins.

EVERYTHING BUT

Now here's a truly dangerous drink. Apart from the alcohol, it also has other exciting ingredients, such as caster sugar, citrus and a whole egg, that only go into the most daring drinks.

No wonder it's called Everything But – the missing words are probably "the Kitchen Sink".

It's actually more of a joke drink than a serious one. When you ask a guest what he wants and he says, "Everything", this is it.

Here goes.

Ice cubes

One part rye whiskey

One part dry gin

One part lemon juice

One part orange juice

One egg

Half a part apricot brandy

One teaspoon of caster sugar

◆ Place six ice cubes in a cocktail shaker and add the whiskey, gin, lemon and orange juice, the egg, apricot brandy and sugar to taste.

◆ Shake very well until smooth and velvety and strain into a highball glass. Add ice cubes if required.

◆ If you really want to go the whole hog, frost the rim of the glass with caster sugar before pouring the drink.

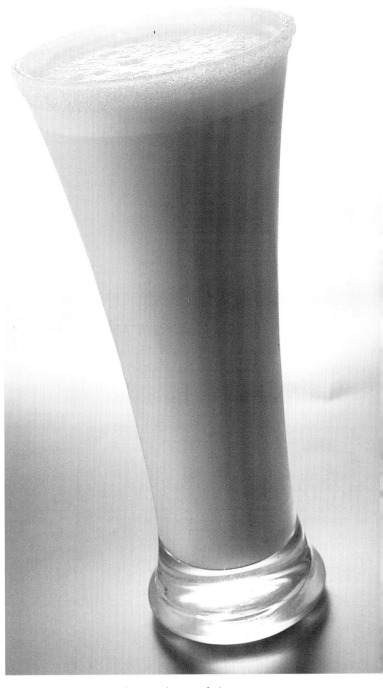

Everything But combines three of the most popular (and very alcoholic) cocktail spirits – gin, whiskey and apricot brandy – all in one power-packed drink.

Dom Pedro (above left), a stunningly simple combination of ice cream and whisky. Irish Coffee (above right) was originally created by the bartender at Shannon Airport near the Irish coast in the late 1940s.

IRISH COFFEE

This is a fine alternative to ordinary coffee at the end of a good meal. The Irish have long been putting a dash of whiskey in their tea and calling it Irish tea, but the barman changed the recipe slightly to appeal to the American airmen who were using Shannon Airport as their base during World War II. Americans have always preferred coffee to tea.

You can actually buy an Irish liqueur called Irish Velvet, which is based on Irish whiskey, black coffee and sugar. It's not as pleasant, or as much fun, as making your own.

One part Irish whiskey

Five parts strong, black coffee

A teaspoon of brown sugar

One part thick cream

* Pour the Irish whiskey and hot coffee into a warmed Irish coffee glass, which is sometimes a goblet with a handle like a teacup and sometimes shaped like a large wineglass.
* Add brown sugar to taste and stir gently until it is dissolved.
* Trickle the cream over the back of a teaspoon onto the surface of the coffee.

The end of an expensive evening (right) as Dolores Costello and Warren William toast each other in Expensive Women.

DOM PEDRO

This has become a firm favourite in South Africa and appears there on many restaurant menus. The strange thing about it is that nobody seems to know who Dom Pedro was or how this sweet delight got its name. There are two basic versions, one using whisky and the other using Kahlua. Both are delicious.

Vanilla ice cream

A generous measure of whisky or Kahlua

Chocolate vermicelli

* Fill a lowball glass or goblet with soft vanilla ice cream and pour the whisky or Kahlua over it.
* Whip briskly with a fork until well blended and serve garnished with a sprinkling of chocolate vermicelli. It is usual to provide a long bar spoon to help reach the bottom bits.

THE BOILERMAKER

It could be argued that this rough-and-ready drink is not a cocktail, as it is taken in two parts. It certainly is a mixed drink, though. I've seen it drunk in several countries, by drinkers in various stages of alcoholic merriment.

A shot glass of blended whisky
A mug of lager beer

◆ The shot glass of whisky is usually swallowed in a single gulp, followed by a glass of beer. Sometimes the whisky and beer are mixed in a glass or tankard and drunk together.

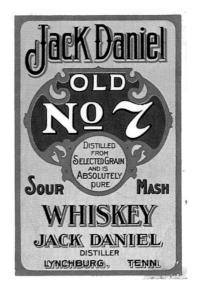

An early label (above) from the Jack Daniel Distillery, which in 1866 became the first registered distillery in America.

The boilermaker – not a drink for the faint-hearted.

WHITE HEATHER

Bartenders throughout the world compete regularly at international gatherings, where new drinks are tried, discussed and judged. This award-winning recipe, invented by barman Rodney Brock, specified the brand of each of the ingredients, but we leave it to readers to select their own. It really is a wonderful drink.

Ice cubes

One part Scotch whisky

One part crème de banane

One part crème de cacao

Two parts thin cream

Nutmeg

The White Heather (above left) *won an award in Hamburg, Germany in 1984. The egg white added to the Rattlesnake* (above right) *gives it its silky texture.*

◈ Place three ice cubes in a cocktail shaker and add all the ingredients except the nutmeg.

◈ Shake well and strain into a cocktail glass.

◈ Grate nutmeg over the drink and serve.

RATTLESNAKE

One of the many slang names for illicit moonshine liquor was "snake juice", which probably referred to the rough mountain-distilled spirit. This is a refined version, using bourbon.

Crushed ice

Two parts bourbon

One teaspoon of lemon juice

One teaspoon of sugar syrup

Half an egg white

Several dashes of Pernod

◈ Place a scoop of crushed ice in a cocktail shaker and add the bourbon, lemon juice, sugar syrup, egg white and Pernod.

◈ Shake vigorously for 10 seconds or more and strain it into a chilled lowball glass.

" I always carry a little Whisky with me in case I see a snake.
I always carry a snake as well."

W. C. Fields

CHAMPAGNE
& WINE

Many purists will be horrified at the thought of adding anything to wine, considered by the faithful to

be an almost sacred drink. Even an ice cube in a glass of Chardonnay raises the eyebrows of the purists.

But we shouldn't worry too much about fanatics.

Wine, sparkling or still, has been used in all sorts of mixtures for centuries. Like so many of life's

pleasures, wine mixtures were often born of necessity. On freezing cold European winter evenings, a

mug of steaming mulled wine was a real comfort. Before the discovery of the cork stopper, wines did

not last as long as they do today. Red wine stored in a barrel or amphora sealed with a wooden stopper

wrapped in linen would turn to vinegar after a year or so, and needed all the help it could get.

A selection of warming spices did the trick, and Glühweins and Glöggs were born.

The Greeks sealed their wine jars with wooden stoppers and poured melted resin over them to keep

out the air. Obviously some resin got into the wine and made retsina. Today it's almost the national drink of Greece and the resin is added deliberately, although the need for wooden stoppers is long past.

The French, who would not think of enjoying a meal without wine, bring up their children on watered wine until they are old enough to drink it neat. And if you're happy to dilute it with water, why not with something else?

Champagne has been called the king of wines, and like all good rulers, it mixes comfortably with all manner of lesser subjects. Small wonder that so many champagne-based drinks contain the word "royal" in their names.

It can be combined with almost any liqueur or fruit juice to create a wide range of exciting cocktails, and is said to be the only wine that may acceptably be served at breakfast.

WINE COLLINS

As with many successful drinks, this one depends on achieving just the right balance between sweet and sour. It uses a sweet wine as a base, balancing the sweetness with the juice of a fresh lime.

Ice cubes
Four parts Madeira, Marsala or ruby port
Half a part fresh lime juice
Dry lemon drink
A maraschino cherry

◆ Place four ice cubes in a mixing glass and add the wine and lime juice. Stir well and strain into a lowball glass.

◆ Top up with the dry lemon drink. Stir lightly to retain the sparkle and garnish with the cherry on a stick.

Experiment with proportions to create your own version of the Wine Collins.

WALTZING MATILDA

Here's a good summer cooler.

Crushed ice
Four parts dry white wine
One part gin
One part passion fruit juice
Half a teaspoon of Curaçao
Soda water or ginger ale according to your taste
Orange peel

❖ Place a scoop of crushed ice in a cocktail shaker and add the wine, gin, passion fruit juice (you could use passion fruit cordial if the real thing is not available) and the Curaçao.

❖ Shake briskly, then strain the contents into a highball glass.

❖ Top up with the sparkling mixer of your choice and garnish with a twist of orange peel.

SHERRY SHANDY

Here's a refreshing summer drink that can be made as concentrated or as weak as you please.

Three dashes of Angostura bitters
Two sherry glasses of amontillado sherry
A bottle of ginger ale or ginger beer
Ice cubes
A slice of lemon

❖ Splash the bitters into a chilled highball glass and swirl it around to coat the inside of the glass.

❖ Pour in the sherry and fill the glass with the ginger ale or ginger beer.

❖ Float an ice cube on the top and serve garnished with a slice of lemon.

Waltzing Matilda (right), as the name suggests, was invented in the dusty outback of Australia.

MULLED CLARET

Mulled wine has been a traditional winter drink for centuries. Modern recipes, compared with those of days gone by, are slightly more refined, better tasting and certainly with more of a kick.

The peel of a lemon
Six whole cloves
Ground cinnamon to taste
A pinch of grated nutmeg
Five parts red Bordeaux-style wine
One part ruby port
One part brandy

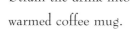

- Place the lemon peel, cloves, cinnamon and nutmeg in a saucepan, add the liquid ingredients and heat slowly until almost, but not quite, boiling. If it is allowed to boil it loses its alcohol.
- Strain the drink into a warmed coffee mug.

Mulled Claret (right) *is a more refined version of the traditional winter drink, originally made simply by heating a fire poker and plunging it into a tankard of wine.*

SANGRIA

Sangria is one of the old traditional punches, much enjoyed in Spanish-speaking countries. The name is derived from the Spanish "sangre", meaning blood, and obviously refers to its colour. There are almost as many recipes for sangria as there are for martinis. Interestingly, sangria is one of the few punches that is made as an individual drink as well as a communal cocktail. We have used large quantities here, but you can scale them down to suit your own needs.

A nice touch is to serve the sangria in a goblet with a sugar-frosted rim. It turns the drink into a really special occasion.

Two bottles of red wine
Half a cup of Curaçao
Half a cup of brandy
The juice of an orange
The juice of a lemon or lime
Half a cup of caster sugar (or to taste)
A chunk of ice
Orange, peach and lemon slices
A small bottle of soda water (optional)

- Mix all the liquid ingredients, except the soda water.
- Add the caster sugar and strain into a punch bowl containing a chunk of ice.
- Garnish with the fruit slices.
- Add the soda water shortly before serving.

Quite apart from being a delicious, silky-smooth drink, the Sherry Eggnog is reputed to be soothing for a sore throat and helpful for a hangover.

"Indeed, indeed, repentance oft before
I swore – but was I **sober** when I **swore?**"

OMAR KHAYYAM

SHERRY EGGNOG

The Sherry Eggnog is a smooth and sensual drink with a velvety texture.

Crushed ice

Two sherry glasses of amontillado sherry

A dessertspoon of caster sugar (or to taste)

A fresh egg

A cup of milk

Grated nutmeg

- Place half a cup of crushed ice in a blender or cocktail shaker. Add the sherry, caster sugar, egg and milk and shake or blend until smooth and velvety.
- Strain into a chilled highball glass and dust with grated nutmeg.

CHAMPAGNE CLASSIC

There are several versions of the Champagne Classic, some of which leave out the brandy. It's a simple and deliciously elegant drink.

A cube of sugar

A dash of Angostura bitters

Chilled dry champagne

A teaspoon of brandy

A cocktail cherry

- Place the cube of sugar in a champagne flute and add a dash or two of Angostura bitters.
- Carefully fill the glass with champagne.
- Add the teaspoon of brandy.
- Serve decorated with the cocktail cherry.

BELLINI

The Bellini became the favourite drink of celebrities like Noël Coward and Ernest Hemingway when they visited Harry's Bar in Venice. It's easy to see why.

Modern bartenders may be tempted to use the readily available canned or boxed peach juice for this drink, but the real connoisseur would never accept anything but the fresh juice of ripe peaches. It really is worth the extra effort.

Peel several ripe peaches and remove the stones. Place them in a blender and whip them to a smooth purée. In his cookbook, Harry's Bar's present owner, Arrigo, says they never used anything as crude as a blender in the "good old days". Small white peaches were squeezed by hand and pushed through a sieve to make the pulp.

One generous part fresh peach juice
Four equally generous parts dry champagne
A peach slice

- Pour the fruit juice into a champagne flute, filling it about a quarter full.
- Top up the glass with champagne. Do not stir or shake.
- Garnish with the peach slice on the rim of the glass and serve.

The Bellini (left) was created in the 1940s by Guiseppe Cipriani, the founder of Harry's Bar in Venice, in honour of the famous Venetian painter, Bellini.

KIR ROYALE

This drink was first named Kir after the war hero and mayor of Dijon, Felix Kir. In smart cocktail bars the rough peasant wine was later replaced with fine champagne and the drink was elevated to royal status. Today Kir is the same drink made with dry white wine, while Kir Royale is the version that uses champagne.

Seven parts chilled dry champagne
One part chilled crème de cassis (or raspberry
 liqueur if you prefer)
A twist of lemon rind

* Fill a champagne flute about three-quarters full with chilled champagne.
* Add the liqueur and serve garnished with the twist of lemon rind.

"I DRINK when I have occasion for it, and sometimes when I have not."

Don Quixote

Kir Royale (right), an old classic, is said to have been made originally by Burgundian farm labourers who were given rather indifferent wines to drink, and decided to improve the flavour by adding blackcurrant juice to it.

The Rossini (above left), a variation of the Bellini, uses fresh strawberry purée instead of peach juice. Death in the Afternoon (above right) is said to have been a favourite of Ernest Hemingway when he lived in Paris.

ROSSINI

Here's a pretty and refreshing drink to serve when strawberries are in season – perfect while watching tennis at Wimbledon.

One part puréed strawberries
Three parts dry sparkling wine
One fresh strawberry

◆ Pour the strawberry purée into a champagne flute and top up with chilled sparkling wine. Stir very gently, trying not to dissipate the bubbles.
◆ Float the fresh strawberry on top and serve.

DEATH IN THE AFTERNOON

Like many of the champagne-based cocktails, it requires very gentle handling to retain the delicate bubbles.

Ice cubes
One part Pernod
Chilled dry champagne

◆ Place two ice cubes in the bottom of a champagne flute and add the Pernod.
◆ Slowly pour in champagne to fill the glass, then stir very gently so as not to lose the sparkle.
◆ Serve ungarnished.

Alexander Kirkland offers Irene Ward an olive in Humanity.

The art of sabrage – decapitating a bottle of champagne with a sabre – can still be used to start a party with a bang, but practise in private first.

"**Drinking** makes such FOOLS OF PEOPLE, and people are such **fools** to begin with that it's compounding a felony."

Robert Benchley

BLACK VELVET

It's not difficult to see how this old favourite got its name. A good stout has a smooth, creamy consistency rather like liquid velvet, and the sparkling wine adds a special glow.

The drink is said to have been created in Brooks' London Club in 1861 when Queen Victoria and all of Britain was in mourning for Prince Albert. The barman created this solemn drink using Guinness stout and champagne.

A bottle or can of
  Guinness stout
A bottle of dry
  champagne

- Half-fill the glass with the stout, then gently pour in the champagne, trying to create as little foam as possible.
- Serve without ice or garnish.

Black Velvet (right) is traditionally served in a beer tankard, but in modern, more refined times, a champagne flute is often used instead.

CHAMPAGNE BLUES

This dramatic drink was created by barman and author John J. Poister as a tribute to the authors of *Champagne Blues*, Nan and Ivan Lyons. They say it's impossible to have the blues when you're drinking champagne, so maybe we should take note of this as a remedy for depression.

Dry champagne
Blue Curaçao
Lemon peel

◆ Pour the chilled champagne into a chilled tulip glass and add the blue Curaçao to taste.
◆ Twist the lemon peel over the drink to release the zest and drop it into the glass as a garnish. Cheer up.

PRINCE OF WALES

Here's another champagne-based drink with a royal connection. It was probably a favourite of Queen Victoria's son, Alfred, who seems to have led a merry life as he toured about the British Empire.

Ice cubes
One part brandy
One part Madeira or any sweet, fortified
  white wine
Three drops of Curaçao
Two dashes of Angostura bitters
Chilled dry champagne
A slice of orange

◆ Place five ice cubes in a cocktail shaker and add the brandy, sweet wine, Curaçao and Angostura bitters.
◆ Shake well and strain into a tall champagne flute. Fill it gently with champagne and garnish it with a slice of orange.

BUCK'S FIZZ

Probably the most common of all champagne-based drinks, Buck's Fizz is now served regularly at champagne breakfasts and celebrity lunches. It is an ideal early-morning drink, as it can be made as strong or as weak as you please and is certainly very invigorating. It is said to have been invented by the barman at Buck's Club in London in the 1920s. You can now buy Buck's Fizz ready-mixed in a champagne-type bottle or even in a can, but it will never replace the real thing.

One part fresh orange juice
Two parts chilled champagne or dry sparkling
  wine

◆ Pour about one-third of a champagne flute full of orange juice and top up with champagne. Stir gently, so as not to dissipate all the bubbles, and serve.
◆ For added fun, the champagne flute can have its rim frosted with sugar.

From left to right: *Champagne Blues, Prince of Wales, Buck's Fizz and Southern Champagne, four classic, champagne-based cocktails.*

SOUTHERN CHAMPAGNE

Southern Comfort is a pleasantly warming drink that can be used in many combinations to create interesting cocktails. Here it is used to add a whole new dimension to dry champagne.

Angostura bitters

One shot glass of Southern Comfort

Dry champagne

Orange peel

- Splash a dash or two of Angostura bitters into a champagne flute and swirl it about to coat the inside.
- Pour in the Southern Comfort and top up with chilled dry champagne. Do not stir.
- Twist the orange peel over the drink to release the zest and drop the peel into it as a garnish.

FUTURE CLASSICS

Most drinkers tend to be conservative in their daily drinking habits, ordering the same drink and the same

brand time after time. Cocktails have changed all that and drinkers are now more likely to be adven-

turous and try new drinks and new combinations of drinks.

The liquor industry is a vibrant and competitive one and new and exciting drinks are released on

the market every year. As can be expected, this brings an annual crop of new cocktails as bartenders

around the world see what magic they can weave with the new flavours. Some of these newcomers are

great, others merely good.

Some of the cocktails on the following pages will enjoy a brief spell of fame and then fade from the

scene forever. Others may go on to become classics like the Martini and the Harvey Wallbanger. We

leave it to readers to make up their own minds as to which will stay and which will fade from memory.

THE GREEK TIGER

This variation of the classic cocktail called the Tiger Tail was offered to me on a ferry from Athens to Poros. The ship's steward insisted it was the perfect way to introduce a foreigner to the delights of ouzo. I had to agree.

Ice cubes
Four parts fresh orange juice
One part ouzo
A slice of lime
A twist of lime peel

 ◆ Place four ice cubes in a cocktail shaker and add the orange juice and ouzo.
 ◆ Shake well and strain into a cocktail glass.
 ◆ Squeeze the slice of lime over the drink and decorate it with the lime peel.

FRANGELICO LUAU

Frangelico is reputed to have been created by an Italian hermit three centuries ago and is a delicious liqueur made from hazelnuts and berries. It is the base for many unusual and complex-flavoured cocktails like this one.

One part Frangelico liqueur
Four parts fresh pineapple juice
A dash of grenadine
Ice cubes
Fresh pineapple

 ◆ Pour the Frangelico, pineapple juice and grenadine into a blender and blend for about 10 seconds. Pour into a chilled tall glass and add three ice cubes.
 ◆ Decorate with a slice of fresh pineapple.

Frangelico Luau (left)
provides a rich
combination of fruit, berry
and nut flavours.

THE PINK SQUIRREL

Any drink that's flavoured with nut liqueur and decorated with nuts is likely to find itself branded as a squirrel's favourite.

Crushed ice
One part crème de noyaux or Frangelico liqueur
One part crème de cacao
One part thin cream
Half a walnut

* Place a few spoons of crushed ice in a cocktail shaker or blender. Add the nut liqueur, crème de cacao and cream and shake or blend thoroughly.
* Strain into a cocktail glass and serve with the walnut half floating on the surface.

Like the limousine it was named after, the Golden Cadillac is a slick and smooth creation.

The Pink Squirrel is a cheeky little drink with a nutty character and is as smooth as a squirrel's fur.

GOLDEN CADILLAC

Galliano has a vivid golden colour and a nutty-sweet flavour. The crème de cacao gives a smooth chocolaty flavour and the cream allows it to slip down like liquid velvet.

Ice cubes
One part Galliano
One part crème de cacao
One part thin cream

* Place three ice cubes in a cocktail shaker and add the Galliano, crème de cacao and cream.
* Shake well and strain into a cocktail glass.
* Serve ungarnished.

TEQUILA SUNRISE

Tequila, of course, is the national drink of Mexico, and this cocktail is one of many based on the fiery spirit. It has become a cocktail classic.

One part tequila
Three parts fresh orange juice
Two dashes of grenadine
A maraschino cherry

◆ Pour the tequila and orange juice into a high-ball glass and stir them well.
◆ Splash the grenadine on top of the mixture, close to the side of the glass, and watch the colour sink gently through the drink.
◆ Garnish with a cherry on a cocktail stick.

The Tequila Sunrise (left) gets its name from its stunning appearance. Tequila (above) is a spirit distilled from the agave cactus and forms the basis of many well-known cocktails.

The Margarita, probably the best known of all tequila-based drinks, is traditionally served in a salt-rimmed cocktail glass.

MARGARITA

Nobody remembers who Margarita was, but her name lives on in this fiery little drink which can be served straight up or frozen.

Crushed ice

Three parts tequila

One part Triple Sec

One part lime juice (preferably fresh)

Salt

Ice cubes

◈ Place a scoop of crushed ice in a blender or shaker and add the tequila, Triple Sec and lime juice. Blend or shake well.

◈ Dip the rim of a cocktail glass in egg white or lemon juice and frost with salt.

◈ Add two ice cubes and gently pour the Margarita mixture over them, taking care not to disturb the salt frosting.

The Golden Dream (above left) was invented when Galliano came onto the market in 1960. *The smooth, minty flavour of Grasshopper (above right)* is just right to clear the palate after a good meal.

THE GRASSHOPPER

This is a different and exciting drink, both in looks and flavour. The mint and coffee flavours are traditional meal-enders, so what better than combining them in an attractive drink?

The cream gives it a silky texture. A well-rounded cocktail.

Ice cubes

One part green crème de menthe

One part crème de cacao

One part thin cream

- Place three ice cubes in a cocktail shaker and add all the other ingredients.
- Shake well and strain into a cocktail glass.
- Serve ungarnished or with a sprig of mint.

GOLDEN DREAM

Bartenders and mixologists everywhere recognised Galliano's potential as a cocktail ingredient and there was a rush to see who could use it to best advantage. This delightful concoction certainly deserves an award for flavour and looks.

Ice cubes
Two parts Galliano
One part Cointreau
One part fresh orange juice
One part thin cream

- Place three ice cubes in a cocktail shaker and add the Galliano, Cointreau, orange juice and cream.
- Shake vigorously, then strain the contents into a cocktail glass.
- Serve ungarnished.

MEXICAN RUIN

Tequila has probably been the ruin of many a Mexican, but this elegant variation should not leave too wide a trail of destruction in its wake.

Crushed ice
One part tequila
One part coffee liqueur

- Place a scoop of crushed ice in a cocktail mixing glass.
- Add the tequila and coffee liqueur and stir well.
- Strain into a cocktail glass and serve.

"I've made it a rule **never**

to drink by daylight and

never to refuse

a drink after DARK."

H. L. Mencken

The Mexican Ruin is good with coffee, or even instead of coffee.

Bebe Daniels drains her drink as Julia Faye and William Boyd look on in Nice People.

The Montezuma (above left), in which egg yolk is used to create the golden hue, and TNT (above right), a drink with a potentially explosive result.

MONTEZUMA

Mexico again, and this time it's a really unusual drink that looks good and tastes wonderful.

Crushed ice (or ice cubes if using a shaker)
One egg yolk
Two parts tequila
One part Madeira wine

◈ Place a scoop of crushed ice in a blender (or four ice cubes in a cocktail shaker) and add the egg yolk, tequila and Madeira wine.
◈ Blend for about 15 seconds, or shake very vigorously, and strain the drink into a chilled cocktail glass.

TNT (TEQUILA 'N' TONIC)

Anything based on tequila is likely to produce interesting results. This one's not a drink for the faint-hearted.

Ice cubes
Two parts tequila
Half a part fresh lime juice
Tonic water
Lemon peel

◈ Place three ice cubes in a bar glass, add the tequila and lime juice and stir well.
◈ Strain into a lowball glass, top up with tonic water and garnish with a twist of lemon peel.

DANISH MARY

In the chilly Scandinavian countries they distill a robust liquor called aquavit. It is made from potatoes or grain and lightly flavoured with caraway and other seeds. Traditionally it is enjoyed neat and swallowed in a single gulp, but it can also be used in some good cocktails.

Ice cubes

One part aquavit

One small can of tomato juice

Two dashes of Worcestershire sauce

Lemon juice

Celery salt

A celery stick

◆ Place four or five ice cubes in a cocktail shaker and add the aquavit, tomato juice, Worcestershire sauce, a few teaspoons of lemon juice and a dusting of celery salt.

◆ Shake well and strain into a highball glass.

◆ Garnish with the stick of celery and serve.

THE FROZEN MATADOR

Bullfighting usually takes place in the heat and dust of summer, so there is something rare and unusual about a frozen matador, just as there is about this very refreshing cocktail.

Crushed ice

One part tequila

One part fresh pineapple juice

A dash of fresh lime juice

Ice cubes

Slices of pineapple

Mint leaves

◆ For this drink a blender is essential. Place two generous scoops of crushed ice in the blender and add the tequila, pineapple juice and lime juice. Blend to a frothy mixture.

◆ Strain into a lowball glass, add two ice cubes and garnish with the pineapple slices and the mint leaves.

"We'll teach you to drink ere you depart."

William Shakespeare, *Hamlet*

The Frozen Matador (above left) is a chilly concoction of tequila, pineapple and lime juice. The Danish Mary (above right) is a Bloody Mary made with aquavit instead of vodka.

SHOOTERS

Shooters add a splash of colour to any party. They're sassy and flashy and just a bit daring.

Originally invented by a Canadian barman to keep out the cold, shooters consist of small, high-powered drinks, usually built up in layers of contrasting colour and designed to be knocked back in a single gulp. The art of making a shooter lies in getting each colour to be cleanly separated from the others. This requires some experimentation if you are to get it right every time, but practice makes perfect.

As a general rule, drinks with a high alcohol content are lighter than those with a lower alcohol content, so they will tend to float on top. In most countries it is required by law to state the alcohol content of the drink on the label, so this gives the budding bartender a good starting point.

This rule does not always apply, though, as some drinks have ingredients that are heavier than the alcohol, but it can be used as a general rule of thumb. It often helps to trickle the top layer onto the lower one by running the drink gently over the back of a teaspoon.

Passionate purple and red, the Love Bite should ideally be made in pairs, so that lovers can toast each other.

LOVE BITE

A romantic little stinger for lovers.

One part cherry liqueur
One part parfait amour liqueur
One part sweet thick cream

◆ Pour the cherry liqueur into the bottom of a shot glass, filling it to about one-third. Carefully trickle the parfait amour onto the surface to fill the glass to about two-thirds.

◆ Finally, slide a layer of sweet cream over the back of a spoon onto the surface and serve.

GALLIANO HOT SHOT

Galliano is a sweet, golden drink that goes well with the coffee or pudding at the end of a good meal. It seems natural to combine it with strong, bitter coffee to create this intriguing taste combination. If the coffee is very hot, it may be advisable to sip this drink, rather than tossing it back in a single gulp.

One part Galliano
One part very strong, hot coffee
Thick cream

- Half-fill a shot glass with Galliano and carefully trickle about the same quantity of hot coffee over the back of a teaspoon to form a dark layer on it.
- Finally, add a topping of cream, sliding it carefully onto the surface of the coffee.

Galliano Hot Shot (above front) *is an intriguing combination of Galliano and hot coffee. The Cactus Flower* (above left), *a searing combination of tequila and Tabasco sauce, is best accompanied by a glass of iced water.*

Galliano (above) *is a golden-hued Italian liqueur that is used in many well-known cocktails, in particular the Harvey Wallbanger* (page 88).

CACTUS FLOWER

Here's a drink for the macho man. Keep a glass of iced water close at hand to douse any flames!

Tabasco sauce
Tequila

- Trickle a generous layer of Tabasco sauce onto the bottom of a shot glass.
- Carefully fill the glass with tequila, trying not to stir up the Tabasco.
- Toss back in a single gulp.

Slippery Nipple is believed to be the invention of a bored winemaker whiling away an idle evening in his local pub.

SLIPPERY NIPPLE

Who could resist a drink with a name as seductive as this?

One part black sambuca
One part Bailey's Irish Cream

◆ Pour the sambuca into a shot glass, filling it to about the halfway mark.
◆ Very carefully trickle Bailey's Irish Cream over the back of a spoon onto the sambuca to fill the glass to the brim.
◆ After admiring your handiwork, take a deep breath, raise the glass and toss the contents back in a single, breathtaking gulp.

GREEN AND GOLD

Inspired by the traditional sporting colours of South Africa's national teams, this is an attractive and rather pleasant little shooter.

One part passion fruit syrup
One part green crème de menthe
A teaspoon of ouzo

◆ Pour a little passion fruit syrup into the bottom of a shot glass or liqueur glass. Gently add the crème de menthe without letting the two colours mix.
◆ When the glass is almost full, dribble a teaspoon of ouzo on top of the drink.

The Green and Gold is a South African invention based on the colours of the national rugby team. Like the players it represents, this cocktail has a powerful kick.

POUSSE CAFE

This is actually the original drink on which the shooter idea is based. Like the shooter, the trick is to build the drink carefully, starting with the heaviest and pouring each subsequent one carefully over the back of a bar spoon so each colour remains separate until the glass is tilted for drinking. It demands a steady hand and is one of the very few drinks where looks are considered as important as flavour.

You could design your own using specially selected colours for particular occasions; the national colours of a country for a national holiday, or the colours of a football team's jerseys to celebrate a victory.

Here's a typical pousse café to begin with.

One part grenadine
One part green crème de menthe
One part Galliano
One part kümmel
One part brandy

◈ Into a small, basically cylindrical glass pour each of the ingredients in the order given, trickling them slowly over a spoon onto the surface of the previous layer until a pretty striped effect is achieved. Serve carefully.

Traditionally served after dinner, the Pousse Café (right) can have as many layers of colour as you like.

It takes a steady hand to form a clean dividing line between the ingredients of the Sombrero.

THE SOMBRERO

Here's a cheerful little splash of Mexican magic to get you throwing your hat in the air.

One part Kahlua
One part thick cream

◆ Chill the Kahlua well and pour it into a shot glass.
◆ Trickle the cream onto the Kahlua, letting it run over the back of a spoon.
◆ Serve with a steady hand.

Alan Mowbray pours Frances Dee a drink in a scene from Nice Women.

The Autumn Leaf is an attractive little shooter to drink when welcoming in the season of "mists and mellow fruitfulness".

AUTUMN LEAF

It doesn't matter too much if the colours blend a little. They will end up with the colour of an autumn leaf anyway.

One part green crème de menthe
One part Galliano
One part brandy
Grated nutmeg

- As with other shooters, use a small cylindrical glass and start by pouring in the crème de menthe.
- Now trickle the yellow Galliano carefully on the surface of the green and end off by sliding a layer of golden brandy on top.
- Finish it off with a pinch of nutmeg.

THE BASTILLE BOMB

Fire off this little shooter to celebrate the anniversary of the storming of the Bastille on July 14th, 1789.

One part grenadine
One part blue Curaçao
One part Cointreau

- Start with the grenadine as a base in a small cylindrical glass, then trickle the Cointreau on top of it and round it off with a trickled layer of blue Curaçao. Voila!

The Bastille Bomb comes in the colours of the French tricolor.

A Shot of French Fire (above left) is a good test of dexterity to get the colours separate. In spite of its somewhat inelegant name, the Angel's Tit (above right) has become a classic.

A SHOT OF FRENCH FIRE

Here's a colourful little drink with a French flavour and a cheerful appearance.

One part green chartreuse
One part maraschino liqueur
One part cherry brandy
One part kümmel

- Starting with the chartreuse, trickle each of the ingredients over the back of a spoon into a small, straight-sided glass in the order shown.
- Admire for a few seconds, and toss it down in a single, multi-coloured gulp.

"I have taken more out of alcohol than it has taken out of me."

Winston Churchill

Part of the charm of a shooter is its colourful, layered appearance. Make sure you have a selection of brightly coloured drinks, such a cherry brandy, crème de menthe and green chartreuse, before setting out to create your own rainbow masterpiece.

THE ANGEL'S TIT

It's not difficult to imagine how this creamy, smooth drink, decorated sensuously with a rounded cherry, derived its name. It's one of very few shooters served with a garnish.

One part crème de cacao
One part maraschino liqueur
One part thick cream
A maraschino cherry

- Starting with the crème de cacao, trickle each ingredient into a shooter glass in the order shown.
- Carefully place the cherry in the centre of the cream layer and serve with reverence.

NON-ALCOHOLIC
DRINKS

There are many reasons why some party goers might prefer not to indulge in alcohol. It could be for religious or health reasons, or simply to have one member of the group sober enough to drive the rest home safely, and legally, at the end of the evening. There are also occasions when a party guest might be on some medication that does not combine safely with alcohol.

But these should not be reason to stay away from a good party, or to sit solemnly sipping a glass of water all evening. There are plenty of safe and tasty alcohol-free cocktails around that will provide pleasure without turning the drinker into a party-pooper.

With non-alcoholic drinks, as with any other drink, the secret is to find a good balance between sweetness and acidity. This is why Coco-Cola was such a universal success. It hit just the right balance and stayed with it. When designing any non-alcoholic drink, therefore, the bartender should aim for the same taste balances.

ORANGE FIZZ

Quantities can be varied according to the sweetness of the orange juice. If the mixture is too acidic, add a little sugar to correct the balance.

Ice cubes
One part fresh lime juice
One part fresh lemon juice
Five parts fresh orange juice
Soda water
Sugar to taste (if required)

- Place four ice cubes in a cocktail shaker and add the three fruit juices.
- Shake well and strain into a tall glass.
- Top up with soda water and add a touch of sugar if it is too tart.
- Serve ungarnished.

"For when the wine is in, the WIT is out"

Thomas Becon

The Orange Fizz (left) demonstrates the principle of good balance – it is neither too tart nor too sweet.

VIRGIN MARY

The Virgin Mary is simply a Bloody Mary rendered innocent by the absence of alcohol.

Ice cubes

One can of tomato cocktail

A small measure of lemon juice

A dash of Tabasco sauce per glass

A dash of Worcestershire sauce
  per glass

Celery salt to taste

Pepper

A celery stick

- Place four or five ice cubes in a cocktail shaker and add the tomato cocktail and lemon juice.
- Add the seasonings as required and shake well.
- Strain into a tall glass and serve with the celery stick as a stirrer.

JUNGLE COOLER

Most fruit juices combine well to form interesting flavour combinations. This one is designed to capture the wild exotic character of a tropical jungle.

Crushed ice

Four parts pineapple juice

Two parts fresh orange juice

One part passion fruit squash
  (cordial)

One part coconut milk

A slice of pineapple

Try different fruit juice combinations when making the Jungle Cooler (above left). Sweet and simple, but still delicious, the Virgin Mary (above right) is a Bloody Mary without the vodka.

- Place a cup of crushed ice in a cocktail shaker and add the fruit juices and the coconut milk.
- Shake well and strain into a tall glass.
- Garnish with the slice of pineapple.

JONES'S BEACH COCKTAIL

Cocktails are not necessarily limited to sweet and sour flavours. Some, like the famous Bloody Mary, venture into the savoury taste spectrum. This is another savoury treat.

Crushed ice

A cup of cold beef consommé or a dissolved
  bouillon cube

Half a cup of clam juice

The juice of half a lemon or lime

Half a teaspoon of horseradish sauce

Two dashes of Worcestershire sauce

◆ Place about half a cup of crushed ice in a blender and add all the ingredients except the celery salt.

◆ Blend for about 10 seconds and strain into a highball glass.

◆ Dust with a pinch of celery salt before serving.

PUSSYFOOT

This fun drink should have you purring in no time at all.

Ice cubes

Two parts orange juice

One part lemon juice

Half an egg yolk per glass

A dash of grenadine per glass

A sprig of mint

A cocktail cherry

The Pussyfoot (above) probably got its name from its smooth, silky texture. Fruit (opposite) serves two important functions in a cocktail. It adds appearance and the flavour. A slice of crisp, ripe fruit can provide a tangy touch to an otherwise uninspired drink.

◆ Place four ice cubes in a cocktail shaker and pour all the liquid ingredients over them.

◆ Shake vigorously and strain into a highball glass.

◆ Serve garnished with a sprig of mint, slightly crushed to release the aroma, and a cherry.

BLUE SPARK

Not long ago a catering friend came to me for advice. She had been asked to cater for the annual staff dinner of the national electricity supply organisation and wanted a special cocktail for the occasion. There were two problems. The theme colour for the evening was electric blue (naturally) and many of the staff members were Muslims and were not allowed to drink alcohol. We spent an interesting hour trying various recipes and eventually settled on this one, of which we are both very proud.

Crushed ice
Half a teaspoon of blue food colouring
Two dashes of Angostura bitters
One part lychee juice
Three parts lemonade
A slice of lemon

- Place three spoons of crushed ice in a bar glass, pour in a splash of blue food colouring, the bitters and lychee juice.
- Add the lemonade and stir gently so as not to lose all the bubbles.
- Strain into a lowball glass and garnish with a slice of lemon.

Although the use of food colouring may be considered cheating by the cocktail purists, the Blue Spark (far left) looks very dramatic and tastes wonderful. Here again, the principle of balancing sweet and sour comes to the fore to create the Gentle Sea Breeze (left).

Lew Ayres has a weakness for beautiful girls armed with cocktails in My Weakness.

GENTLE SEA BREEZE

A pleasant and refreshing blend of two fruit juices that really is a treat.

Crushed ice
One part cranberry juice
One part grapefruit juice
Ice cubes
A sprig of mint (optional)

- Place a cup of crushed ice in a blender or cocktail shaker (a blender is best). Add the juices and blend or shake until frothy.
- Pour into a highball glass and add two ice cubes. Serve ungarnished, or with a sprig of mint.

Although a Black Cow is usually made with dark root beer, you can use a cola instead for this recipe.

BLACK COW

In some parts of the world this cocktail is simply known as a "cola special".

Two scoops of vanilla ice cream
A bottle of root beer or cola

◆ Place the ice cream in a highball glass, add the root beer or cola and stir gently.
◆ Serve with a straw and long spoon.

CHERRY POP

Like all good cocktails, alcoholic or not, this one looks good and has a pleasing balance of sweetness and acidity. Vary the proportions to suit your own taste. That's what makes cocktail blending such fun.

One part cherry syrup
Half a part of fresh lemon juice
One part fresh orange juice
Ice cubes
Soda water
A slice of lemon
One glacé cherry

◆ Place the cherry syrup, lemon juice and orange juice in a cocktail shaker and add four cubes of ice.
◆ Shake well and strain into a highball glass.
◆ Top up with soda water and decorate with the slice of lemon and the cherry.

HONEYMOON COCKTAIL

After the wedding reception the bride and groom probably want to keep a clear head as they start their life together.

Crushed ice
A generous part apple juice
An equal part orange juice
A squeeze of lime juice
Two teaspoons of honey
Orange peel
Sugared cherries

◈ Place three spoons of crushed ice in a cocktail shaker and add the apple and orange juice, the squeeze of lime juice and the honey.
◈ Shake well, then strain the mixture into two champagne flutes.
◈ Garnish with a spiral of orange peel and a cherry.
◈ Serve in bed.

"He that goes to bed thirsty rises HEALTHY."

George Herbert

The Honeymoon Cocktail is a lively little cocktail which makes an ideal nightcap for those wanting to keep a clear head.

SHIRLEY TEMPLE

A good drink for anybody who enjoys a really sweet concoction.

Ginger ale
Grenadine syrup
Maraschino cherries

◆ Fill a highball glass with ginger ale and add a splash or two of grenadine syrup.
◆ Stir very gently and drop in three red maraschino cherries.
◆ Serve with a straw.

HONEYSWEET COFFEE

While most cocktails are designed to be enjoyed in the evening, here's one that's fine for any time of day. It even goes well with breakfast.

A teaspoon of clear honey
One mug of freshly brewed, strong coffee
A dash of Angostura bitters
Ice cubes
Whipped cream
Grated nutmeg

◆ Place the honey in the mug of coffee, stir well and allow to chill overnight.
◆ Add the bitters. Now place three ice cubes in a cocktail shaker, add the chilled coffee mixture and shake well.
◆ Strain into a highball glass and float whipped cream on top.
◆ Dust with a pinch of grated nutmeg and serve.

Named after the child actress, the Shirley Temple (above left) became the non-alcoholic cocktail of the 1960s. Honeysweet Coffee (above right) makes a delicious, early-morning drink.

SAFE SEX ON THE BEACH

Like many non-alcoholic cocktails, this one is simply a version of a tried-and-tested recipe without the alcohol. Sex on the Beach uses vodka and fruit schnapps. To make it "safe", we leave out the vodka and replace the fruit schnapps with fruit nectar.

Ice cubes

One part peach nectar

Three parts pineapple juice

Three parts orange juice

A squeeze of fresh lime juice

A twist of lime peel

A slice of kiwi fruit

A strawberry

◈ Place four ice cubes in a cocktail mixing glass and add the peach nectar (usually a blend of peach juice with other, deflavoured fruit juice bases), the pineapple juice, orange juice and the squeeze of lime juice.

◈ Stir it well and strain into a tall glass.

◈ Add fresh ice and garnish with a twist of lime peel, a slice of kiwi fruit and a strawberry.

Safe Sex on the Beach (above left) *is every bit as delicious as the "real thing" while taking away that morning-after worry. The Catherine Blossom* (above right) *became a classic in the cocktail world as one of the old favourites in the safe drinking list.*

CATHERINE BLOSSOM COCKTAIL

This is deliciously tangy and clean-tasting.

Crushed ice

One cup of fresh orange juice

Two spoons of maple syrup

A dash of lemon juice

A twist of lemon peel

◈ Place two scoops of crushed ice in a blender and add the orange juice, maple syrup and lemon juice.

◈ Blend well and pour into a highball glass.

◈ Garnish with a twist of lemon peel and serve.

GLOSSARY

As with any specialised field of activity, cocktail mixing and bartending in general have developed their own vocabulary. While we have tried to keep jargon to a bare minimum in this book, it's as well to know what people mean when they refer to a drink as being 'straight up' or a *digestif*. Here are some of the more commonly used cocktail terms.

Apéritif: A drink served before a meal to stimulate the appetite. Traditional apéritifs include fino sherry and brut champagne. Some cocktails are made dry for the same reason.

Bar syrup: A sweetening agent, usually made by mixing three parts sugar to one part water. A well-equipped bar always has a bottle of ready-made bar syrup handy.

Blend: In modern cocktail bars an electric blender has become standard equipment. It is particularly useful when fresh fruit is to be puréed as part of a drink. To blend a drink, run the machine for only about 10 seconds.

Dash: A dash of something is simply a small amount splashed into the glass. Usually very strong flavours, like bitters, sauces or syrups, are added in dashes.

Digestif: A small, usually quite sweet drink served at the end of a meal to aid digestion.

Flip: A flip is a short drink mixed with egg and sometimes sugar and shaken into a smooth froth. A single egg is often too rich for just one flip, and it is difficult to separate an egg into two, so it is easiest to make them two at a time.

Float: To pour a small amount of liquor or cream on top of a cocktail so it does not mix with the rest of the ingredients. This is often done by trickling it over the back of a spoon.

Frappé: A frappé is a drink made by pouring a sweet liqueur over crushed ice. It is served with a straw, so the melting ice and liqueur are sipped together from the bottom of the glass. See also 'Mist'.

Frosting: Glasses can be frosted by wetting the rim with water or egg white and dipping it into sugar, which then clings to the rim. Margaritas are traditionally served in glasses frosted with salt instead of sugar.

Jigger: A small measure used in making cocktails. The American jigger contains 1.5 ounces, or 42.3 cc. There are also one-ounce and two-ounce jiggers.

Mist: A straight (neat) alcoholic liquor poured over crushed ice. A mist is related to a frappé, which is a sweet liqueur poured over crushed ice.

Muddle: Herbs, such as mint, are sometimes muddled to release the juices and flavour. This is done by placing them at the bottom of a glass and crushing them to a smooth paste using a wooden pestle, so as not to scratch the glass. Sometimes bar spoons are made with a flat disc at the end of the long handle. This is designed to be used as a muddler.

Mulled: A drink served hot and usually enjoyed during winter. Originally drinks like ale and wine were warmed by plunging a hot poker into the tankard. As hot pokers are a rarity today, the drinks are simply warmed over a stove or hot plate.

Neat: Served without any mixer or ice. In Scandinavian countries, aquavit is often drunk neat. James Bond sometimes swigs his vodka neat.

On the rocks: Poured over ice cubes. Often a glass is filled to the top with ice cubes and the liquor is then trickled over them. It serves a double purpose: it dilutes the liquor slightly and chills it.

Punch: A punch is a large drink made of liquor and fruits and served from a punch bowl at a large gathering. It's a sort of bulk-delivered cocktail.

Shake: To pour the ingredients into a cocktail shaker with some ice and shake it vigorously to ensure a good blend. The ice acts as a beater and dilutes it slightly.

Spiral: Sometimes a drink calls for a 'spiral' of orange or lemon peel. This is cut from the fruit in a long spiral and used to decorate and flavour the drink.

Straight up: Served without ice, usually in a tall glass.

Strain: After shaking or stirring a drink, you usually want to separate the liquid from the ice or peel or other solid ingredients. To do this, the drink is poured through a strainer. Good bars have specially designed strainers that fit over their shakers or mixing glasses.

Swizzle stick: A stirrer, sometimes made of silver, ivory or wood, but today mostly made of plastic. It acts as a decoration for the drink and can also be used to stir it from time to time. Many liquor companies provide swizzle sticks that bear the company logo or crest on the top.

Twist: A long piece of peel (usually citrus) that is twisted in the middle to release the tangy oil from the outer zest layer. It is then dropped into the drink as a garnish.

Zest: The very outside part of the citrus peel. It is obtained by cutting it off with a sharp knife or vegetable peeler. Zest does not include the soft white part (pith) of the skin.

INDEX